THE ELEMENTS OF A HOME

THE

—Curious Histories behind

ELEMENTS

Everyday Household Objects,

OF A

from Pillows to Forks—

HOME

AMY AZZARITO

CHRONICLE BOOKS

SAN FRANCISCO

For Mark

Copyright © 2020 by **AMY AZZARITO**.

LIBRARY OF CONGRESS CATALOGING-IN-PUBLICATION DATA:

Names: Azzarito, Amy, author.

Title: The elements of a home : curious histories behind everyday household objects, from pillows to forks / Amy Azzarito.

Description: San Francisco, CA : Chronicle Books LLC, [2020] | Includes bibliographical references.

Identifiers: LCCN 2019010793 | ISBN 9781452178721 (hardcover : alk. paper)

Subjects: LCSH: House furnishings--History. | Interior decoration--History. |

Home--History. | Curiosities and wonders.

Classification: LCC TX315 .A99 2020 | DDC 645--dc23 LC record available at https://lccn.loc.gov/2019010793

Manufactured in China.

MIX
Paper from
responsible sources
FSC™ C008047

FSC
www.fsc.org

Design by **RACHEL HARRELL**.
Artwork by **ALICE PATTULLO**.

10 9 8 7 6 5 4 3

Chronicle Books LLC
680 Second Street
San Francisco, CA 94107
www.chroniclebooks.com

Contents

WELCOME HOME

"I've a great respect for *things*!" says Madame Merle in Henry James's *The Portrait of a Lady*, ". . . one's house, one's furniture, one's garments, the books one reads, the company one keeps—these things are all expressive." This is a book about things. The things that fill our homes say a great deal about who we are, as well as what we are and whom we value. Our favorite pieces are imbued with stories: the rocker purchased to soothe a now-grown child, the pewter platter inherited from a favorite grandmother, the sofa purchased for a first apartment.

Every domestic object—the desk I'm writing at, the chair I'm sitting on, the lamp that lights the room—not only has a personal history but also a secret history with roots in the past. Take chairs, for example. Sometimes we can identify the designer and provenance of a particular version, as with the Chiavari or Tolix. Sometimes we know about when a certain variety of chair first appeared—for example, the Windsor or rocking chair—but can't pinpoint an exact date or designer. Still, there's no way to know when the very first chair was built. And for many of these quotidian items, like the desk or the plate, it can be nearly impossible (and often, frankly, uninteresting) to trace their exact moment of creation. In *The Elements of a Home*, I looked for the highlights in objects' lives as they evolved to become the things that are familiar to us today.

Most household objects began their lives to fill a need: something to lie on, sit on, cook in, drink from, chase away the dark. That doesn't mean they were always plain; human beings seem to be drawn to beauty. Once the basic needs of food and shelter were taken care of, people had time to indulge the impulse to decorate their living spaces. Utility became luxury. A crystal goblet becomes valuable as a measure of the time and cost that went into making it. A plain piece of carpet can take the chill off the stone wall of a castle, but a vibrant tapestry says the owner has money to spare.

Until the eighteenth century and the advent of the Industrial Revolution, the decorative arts as we think of them now—objects created to make life aesthetically pleasing as well as to be useful—were almost exclusively the purview of the aristocracy and the wealthy, no matter where you lived. It's worth remembering that the colorful pillows, comfortable mattresses, flatware, and upholstered chairs found in even the most basic of modern homes were once only accessible to society's upper echelons.

Perhaps, like me, you find yourself feeling grateful for our ancestors who suffered with stone or wooden head-rests, stiff-backed chairs, and long, cold, dark days and nights before feather-stuffed pillows, upholstered couches, and candles found their way into everyday life. It's important to remember that objects we take for granted, like napkins, glassware, and clocks, were once as unimaginable as a handheld computer was to our grandparents.

Our temperature-controlled homes filled with comfortable furniture and lights that flick on and off at our command are luxurious beyond the wildest dreams of the kings and queens of yesteryear. To trace the histories of many of the things we take for granted (and some we don't), we will often follow in their footsteps. And don't be surprised if, again and again, the French pop up in these pages, as Edmund White writes in *The Flâneur*: "The French invented the idea of luxe and have always been willing to pay for it . . ." But we will also travel to China, Japan, and Egypt to see what we find there.

So come with me on a journey through history, and discover the complex, colorful, and often surprising story of the domestic objects with which we furnish our homes. It's my hope that you close this book with a new appreciation for the quotidian items that occupy your domestic sphere. Or at least have a few new anecdotes for your next dinner party.

Bathtub

If your idea of heaven is a long soak in a hot tub redolent of flowers, you'd feel right at home in the Royal Palace of Mari in Mesopotamia, modern-day Syria. Built more than three thousand years ago, the palace contained the earliest known private bathing room. The multiroom suite featured a shower and two sunken tubs. The queen washed herself in one bathtub, then settled into the other to soak in water scented by perfumed oils.

Skipping forward a millennium or so, the bathhouses of Rome took the luxury of Mesopotamia to the nth degree. The Romans were head over heels in love with bathing, which was a public activity for both rich and poor. Of all the things they built—coliseums, basilicas, bridges—their public baths, marvels of technology and design, were arguably their greatest achievement. Utilizing sophisticated plumbing and heating techniques (including heated floors), these elaborate complexes were imposing structures featuring hot baths, tepid baths, cold baths, and open-air swimming pools. Water poured from silver taps, walls were clad in marble, and mosaics were everywhere—even on the ceilings and the bottom of the bathing pools.

After the fall of the Roman Empire, Europeans continued to enjoy a communal bath. But instead of mosaic-lined pools and marble arches, they bathed in wooden tubs similar to large

THE OFURO

• • • • • • • • • • • •

Bathing is an integral part of Japanese culture. You can find the ofuro—*a square, deep bathtub that was originally made of lemon-scented hinoki wood—in private homes and communal bathhouses. (Today, you can also find plastic or stainless steel versions.) Japanese bathing etiquette demands that you scrub yourself and rinse thoroughly before submerging yourself up to your neck in scalding hot water, which is used by more than one bather. It's a process not to be rushed, a ritual that is intended to cleanse and rejuvenate the spirit as well as the body.*

barrels. Unfortunately for public health and personal hygiene, the arrival of the plague in the fourteenth century put an end to the bathtub for the next four hundred years. Bathing was believed to dilate the pores and allow harmful substances to enter the body. It wasn't until Enlightenment thinking brought about a renewed understanding of the importance of cleanliness that Europeans gradually (read: modestly) began to dip a toe back into the water. And so began the private bath.

This was an era before most homes had running water (in Paris, running water wasn't available to upper stories of buildings until 1865 on the Right Bank and 1875 on the Left). Filling the tub was hard work—so much so that in the early nineteenth century, a clever entrepreneur capitalized on this with the idea for a bath delivery service. You simply selected your water preference (hot, cold, or mineral), and the filled *bain à domicile* (portable tub) would be delivered to your apartment, along with a robe and towel.

Even with this kind of convenience, and the advent of indoor plumbing in the late 1880s, most respectable Europeans still preferred to wash using a basin and pitcher, or take a sponge bath in a low tub. Though in-home bathtubs existed, they were often associated with a licentious lifestyle. After all, the most luxurious bathtub in Paris belonged to La Paiva, the famous nineteenth-century prostitute. She had two: one was sculpted from a block of yellow onyx and the other was silver with three turquoise faucets (one of which poured champagne).

It wasn't until the end of the Civil War that Americans embraced the innovations in technology that made indoor plumbing available to almost everyone. Their enthusiasm for cleanliness and bathing rivaled that of the Romans. For the young country, cleanliness became about asserting class distinctions. The first modern bathtubs were

BOMBS AWAY

· · · · · · · · · · · ·

To preserve a woman's modesty, bathwater was sometimes clouded with powdered almond paste, bran, or milk—a precursor to the modern bath bomb. Women also wore a bathing robe or underwear in the water. Marie-Antoinette, never one to do anything by half measures, did both. Each morning, a copper tub was rolled into her bedroom and filled with a mixture of sweet almonds, pine nuts, linseed, marshmallow root, and lily bulb created by her perfumer, Fargeon. She stepped in wearing a long-sleeve chemise made of English flannel that buttoned at the collar and cuff. Instead of taking her morning meal in bed, she sipped her breakfast of hot chocolate, flavored with orange blossom and topped with whipped cream, while she soaked. Not a bad way to begin the day.

manufactured from enameled cast iron. The porcelain enamel created a smooth interior that would not be corroded by hot water. Kohler introduced their first claw-foot tub in 1873; it carried a hefty $200 price tag (equivalent to $5,000 today). But with improvements in manufacturing and technology, prices dropped dramatically throughout the twentieth century. By 1940, an entire bathroom suite—sink, bath, and toilet—could be purchased for $70 ($1,000 today).

The falling prices of bathroom fixtures and exploding design options were just the beginning. Today, the choices of size, price, materials, and accessories are mind-boggling. Whether you're indulging in a spa-inspired soak and a glass of wine, or going retro with Mr. Bubble and a rubber ducky, you can't go wrong.

Billiard Table

The game of billiards may bring to mind a smoke-filled hall full of two-bit hustlers. Or a wood-paneled room filled with men and women in evening clothes exchanging *bon mots* while they make effortless bank shots. But if you want to know where the game began, you need to head outdoors.

Billiards originated as a ground game in which players used sticks to push balls through obstacles formed by cones, posts, and arches. The origins of this game can be traced all the way back to ancient Egypt, and variations were played in one form or another almost continuously until the Middle Ages. During that tumultuous period, people built houses behind city walls and close to one another for protection from invaders. While the occupants were safer, the area for recreation was greatly reduced. Games once played on expansive fields were adapted to fit the limited space, giving rise to diversions like croquet and bocce. By the early fourteenth century, ground billiards was played in courtyards, enclosures, and sunken terraces specially designed for that purpose.

The first person who became fed up with constantly having to bend down to pick up the ball has been lost to history. But it was in the atmosphere of the refined gentility of the Renaissance that a member of the nobility must have decided to spare his back. Soon, all billiard games played in palaces and monasteries took place on the surface of a table. The equipment became more elevated, too, with game tables decorated with intricate carvings and outfitted with ivory balls, ivory-headed sticks, and brass or silver arches.

To muffle the sound of the balls hitting the wooden surface, a cloth was thrown over the table. Green, which harked back to billiards' origin as a lawn game, was the preferred color—and it remains so today. In the 1500s, a creative gamer was inspired to cut pockets into the hanging edges of the tablecloth to catch wayward balls.

In the late 1400s, Louis XI brought the first billiard table into the French court; it never left (at least not until the monarchy did following the French Revolution). To stay in favor, the king's courtiers began taking billiards lessons on the sly just to stay competitive. Two hundred years later, Louis XIV was completely head over heels for the game. Nearly every evening, he would make his way down the corridors of his beloved Versailles to the *Salon de Diane*. At the room's center was a billiard table covered in red velvet (to match the red soles of Louis's shoes) and trimmed in gold fringe. The room was known as the "chamber of applause" due to the enthusiastic clapping from the court ladies every time the king made a good stroke.

But billiards wasn't just a kingly pastime; ladies got in on the action, too. Of all the injustices that she suffered during her captivity in England, Mary, Queen of Scots, complained most bitterly that her billiard table had been taken from her. Marie-Antoinette had a table that could be raised and lowered installed in her private dining room, and she played with Louis XVI on the eve of her imprisonment. (She won, as was usual. Her secret weapon was a billiard stick made from a single elephant's tusk with a solid gold tip.) And Russian empress Catherine the Great had a billiard table made of maple, inlaid with mother-of-pearl designs.

It was because of those women that the billiard table became a fixture of nineteenth-century mansions throughout Europe and America. While respectable men could play the game in a public tavern, coffee house, or pool hall, a *lady* certainly did not. But even in polite English society, both men and women competed; it was the perfect way to show off a trim waist and fit arms. And

so tables began to be installed inside homes. A round of billiards was standard post-dinner entertainment. Of the grand country houses built in Britain in the nineteenth century, more than two-thirds had a billiards room (most with an adjoining smoking room).

By the early twentieth century, the pool hall had become associated with drunkenness, gambling, and bad behavior. In America, the game itself was thought to lead men and boys down the primrose path of wickedness. By the 1950s, the pool hall and those who frequented it, like Paul Newman's character in *The Hustler*, had become the epitome of working-class cool. Today, pool halls have acquired a retro appeal, not unlike craft cocktails, and the private billiard table has become a status symbol. In Hollywood, a billiard table is nearly as de rigueur in a mogul or movie star's home as it was in a British country estate or a French palace. While billiards has also become associated with hustlers, bars, and a kind of louche subculture, it retains a luxurious mystique, in part because a pool table is an expensive—and hard to move—investment. Maybe it's worth it to play the game of royalty?

What *Is* Billiards, Exactly?

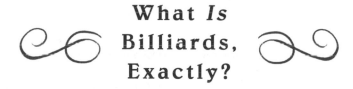

Billiards: The name given to any game played that uses long sticks to direct small balls on a rectangular table. Historically, there were an infinite number of games that fell under the umbrella of billiards. Today, however, the term is likely referring to one of these three:

Carom

Billiards is most commonly played in Western Europe, with three balls on a table without pockets. The idea is to try to score points by caroming the white cue ball into the other two.

Pool

The game you'll likely find throughout the United States. It's played on a table with six pockets. There is one white cue ball, seven striped and seven solid numbered balls, and a black eight ball. The objective is to get all of your seven balls and the black eight ball into the pockets.

Snooker

Played on a six-pocket table with fifteen red and six differently colored balls, and one cue ball. The objective is to use the white cue ball to get the others into the pockets. The player who scores the most points wins the frame, and the player who wins the most frames wins the match. Developed by British Army officers, it's still a U.K. favorite.

Bookshelf

Perusing someone else's bookshelf can feel deliciously voyeuristic, and just as revealing (but not as verboten) as a peek inside their medicine cabinet. But it wasn't so long ago that books were stored in almost every way imaginable *except* for vertical and spine out.

The earliest books had no spines at all. They were scrolls of papyrus. Some readers arranged their collection on shelves fitted with pigeonholes so that the scrolls could be stored flat. Others arranged them so they stood straight up.

In first-century Europe, the codex joined scrolls on the shelves. Composed of papyrus sheets bound between wooden covers, it became the most popular form for presenting text. However, the combination of cylindrical scrolls and hard-covered rectangular codices created an unsightly disorder. The best solution seemed to be to hide the whole mess away in closed cabinets or trunks.

The codex soon supplanted the scroll altogether, but the closed storage system stuck. Books were precious.

Each text had to be laboriously copied by hand, and sometimes covers were inlaid with gold and jewels. Book trunks were often fitted with three locks—the keys held by three different people. Though the system couldn't stop a determined thief, it did deter light-fingered readers.

The downside to book trunks was that they made it impossible to show off a pricey collection. And if you were wealthy enough to have a lot of books, trunks were impractical. Stacked, they blocked natural light, essential for reading before electric lamps were devised. The solution? A room with open shelves and a locked door.

Even with the new open shelves, people continued to store their books as they had their scrolls. Our modern convention of shelving books vertically probably began after horizontal stacks became too unwieldy. With the advent of the printing press, the number of books available increased. So did the size of the stacks. And trying to pull out a tome from the bottom of a tall

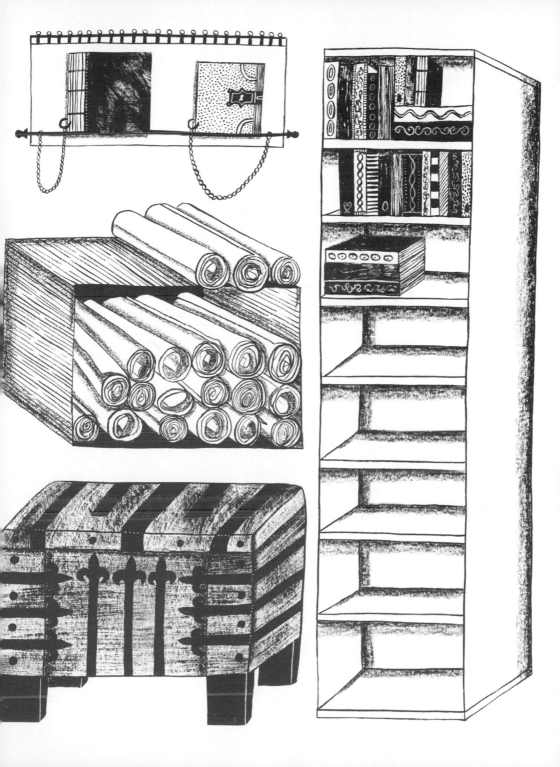

stack was no more fun for the medieval reader than the modern one.

Even once books were organized vertically, most were shelved with the spine facing in. Why? To make sure that they stayed where they belonged. Books in larger collections, particularly monastic libraries, were chained in place, with the chain attached to the spine. By shelving volumes with the fore edges facing out, the book could be taken down and read without tangling the chain. Since you could only take the book the length of the chain, a desk or table had to be brought to the book. Incline desks were built into the bookshelves every few feet.

It was not until 1535, when the first printed spine was created, that books spun on the shelf into the position we're familiar with today. At the time, the fashion in private libraries was to bind all the books in the same leather. An inscribed spine was necessary to distinguish one volume from another.

The enthusiasm for private libraries reached an apex during the Gilded Age. Every New York City mansion seemed to have one. Bibliophiles like American financier J.P. Morgan built elaborate libraries befitting their priceless collections. Morgan's Italian Renaissance–inspired library had three tiers of gilded walnut shelving and an elaborately decorated ceiling (the space is open to the public today as part of the Morgan Library).

until the 1930s, the average person didn't own enough books to need more than a single shelf (or two). That built-in bookshelves made their way into middle-class homes is largely due to the work of Edward Bernays. Known as the "father of public relations," he was the real-life Don Draper and his PR campaigns promoted everything from Dixie cups to Mack trucks. In 1930, he was hired by book publishers to increase sales. His dual-pronged approach used famous public figures to promote the importance of books and simultaneously convinced architects, home contractors, and interior designers to build homes with bookshelves. He was sure that "where there are bookshelves, there will be books."

Swedish furniture powerhouse IKEA began taking care of book lovers in 1979. That was the year designer Gillis Lundgren (the fourth company employee) sketched a bookshelf design on the back of a napkin. He named his design BILLY. Since the first one rolled off the manufacturing line, IKEA has sold more than forty-one million. It remains the company's bestselling item, with fifteen made every minute. With its affordable price point and simple design, BILLY is a favorite of the IKEA hackers—those who like to take an existing product and embellish it. Add moldings and library lights and you've got the built-in look that Edward Bernays made famous. Now you just need to fill it.

Candle

Today, we possess the godlike ability to turn night into day with the flick of a switch. But once upon a time, when the world was a much darker place, candles were both social and economic currency. In an age without electricity, your net worth and status could be calculated by the kind and number of candles you used.

The first factor in that calculation was the candle type. The most rudimentary were rushlights. Used from the time of the ancient Egyptians until the nineteenth century (and even into the twentieth century in some rural areas), these were made by soaking a peeled reed in melted fat. The tall, skinny candles—too fragile to be held upright—were burned in specially made holders that had metal clamps to grip the reed. If properly attended (the flame had to be drawn up through the holder as it burned), a 2-foot- [60-cm-] long rushlight could last for an hour. The rushlight is responsible for the expression "burning the candle at both ends": if you needed a little extra illumination, it could be lit from both sides.

Molded candles were a step up in the candle hierarchy and were also made from animal fat (usually cow or sheep). These cheap homemade candles came at a price for poorer families, who often had to choose whether to eat the fat or use it for illumination. From the time of the Roman Empire, history is filled with stories of starving soldiers eating their candle rations (and the doctors who had to treat the resulting stomach pains).

"All would be horror without candles."

—SIXTEENTH-CENTURY RELIGIOUS MEDITATION

The candles were smelly and smoky, and rotted quickly if left in the open air for too long. Even so, they were used in Great Britain until the twentieth century, albeit to the disgust of many. "Tallow candles," proclaimed Henry Charles Beeching in *Conferences on*

Books and Men, a satirical guide to nineteenth-century high society, "are at all times detestable, and their existence is not even known in genteel life."

The superior candle option was wax, which was prized for its steady white flame (without the animal fat odor!). It is nearly impossible to guess when they were first made, but their use was documented in Rome during the first century. Around the same time in Egypt, wax candles were twisted into a shape that resembled a modern candy cane. In eighth-century Scandinavia, it was a valuable enough commodity that the Norse demanded the Slavs pay a tribute in wax.

E arly wax candles were commonly made of beeswax. Beginning in the early eighteenth century, they were also made from spermaceti, a substance found in the head of the sperm whale; these candles produced a superior, albeit more expensive, light. As a result, the whaling trade exploded. By 1775, the demand for spermaceti created an entire industry, supporting one-hundred fifty whaling vessels in Newport, Rhode Island, alone.

Hosts took illumination seriously. In the 1730s, when English politician Sir Thomas Robinson was invited to a men's-only hunting party at Houghton Hall, the 4,000-acre (1,619-ha), 106-room estate of Prime Minister Sir Robert Walpole, he was so in awe of the number of candles burning in the dining room that he paused to count

FROM CANDLE STUBS TO A MULTIMILLION-DOLLAR BUSINESS

••••••••••••

London's uber-luxurious grocery store Fortnum & Mason owes everything to candles. In the early 1700s, William Fortnum worked as a footman in Kensington Palace. As a perk, employees of the royal family were given half-used candle stubs. (The high-quality candles used in the palace were replaced each night, so there were many leftover ends, which were divided among the staff based on their rank and seniority.) Fortnum sold his share of the discards to the ladies of the court, and by 1707 had saved enough money to start a grocery business with his landlord, Hugh Mason. His business acumen paid off. Today, Fortnum & Mason is the official grocer of the Queen of England, with an annual profit of £88 million (about $115 million).

them. He tallied one-hundred thirty, and in so doing was able to calculate exactly how many British pounds Walpole was sending up in smoke. (About £15 per night, which would be nearly £1,812 or $2,360 today.) For the fashionable set in Georgian London, it wasn't enough to have a massive quantity of candles; they also needed to be of the highest quality, which meant wax—preferably the brighter-burning spermaceti variety. (The candles burning in Houghton Hall were most certainly the real deal.) Cut glass chandeliers, mirrors, gilt furniture, silver flatware—even the sequins and metallic threads woven into party clothes—would reflect light and further illuminate the space.

From the perfumed court of Louis XV to Georgian homes in London, candles were often tasked with scenting the space as well as providing light. The sage-green bayberry candle was a favorite in Europe. Imported from the American colonies, the tapers were made from the fruit of the bayberry shrub, native to the Atlantic coast. When boiled, the berries' waxy coating floated to the top, and this material could be turned into smokeless candles with a clear white flame and a light, pleasant scent.

Even today, some consumers will spend hundreds of dollars for scented candles. Among the most luxurious are those made by the Parisian company Cire Trudon. Founded in the seventeenth century, it has a client roster that spans centuries and includes Napoleon, Madonna, and Catherine Deneuve. Executive director Julien Pruvost explained why the candle stills holds such a magical appeal in an age of electricity. "Taking time in general is probably more and more a luxury nowadays," he told me. "Lighting a scented candle is about taking time to appreciate and care for something that will enhance your environment. Nothing compares to candlelight in an interior."

Canopy Bed

A canopy bed figures high on the wish list of every little girl with fairy-tale princess dreams. It's ranked right up there with a tiara and tulle skirt. Unlike glitter wands and glass slippers, this luxurious bed was a real fixture in the lives of European princesses (and kings and queens).

Crusaders brought the concept of a fabric-encased bed to Europe from the Middle East. The draperies provided much-needed warmth in a chilly castle bedroom. They also bestowed some privacy (visual if not aural) at a time when nobility shared rooms with servants and other sleepers. At first, the curtains of these early canopy beds were suspended from the ceiling by a device that looked like an upside-down bowl. Later, they were hung from rings, which were strung on rods that formed a square around the bed.

Four-poster beds became fashionable in the fifteenth century, and by the sixteenth century, the curtains evolved into an elaborate series of draperies that completely covered the frame. When closed, they made the bed look like a big box with feather-festooned finials perched on top. The heavy fabric protected the sleeper from drafts, which were thought to cause disease.

Though it may look familiar to our modern eye, the way the canopy beds were used was decidedly not. In those virtually chair-free days, the bed was the only seating in the room. During the day, the yards of sumptuous fabric were pulled and tied up to form large hanging teardrops that allowed visitors to climb in with their host for a chat (and surprisingly, no thoughts of hanky-panky).

In seventeenth-century France, the epicenter for showstopping excess, the most resplendent canopy was created for the Porcelain Trianon. Built for Louis XIV's rendezvous with his royal mistress Madame de Montespan, the retreat was just a thirty-minute walk from the Palace of Versailles. The centerpiece of the Love Bedroom (its real name!) was a giant canopy bed adorned with garlands of tassels, fabric swags, ribbons, and mirrors inset into the headboard.

CLUB BED

··············

In seventeenth-century China, upper-class women spent much of their day in their bedrooms. The centerpiece was a colorful canopied bed. During the day, the curtains were pulled back so that it could function as a sofa for entertaining friends. Small tables could be placed inside for eating or playing games.

Both the bed and its hangings formed the cornerstone of a woman's dowry, and even if the marriage dissolved, it remained her property.

By the end of the seventeenth century, the whims of fashion had shifted again. Four-poster beds were replaced by flying testers—named because canopies appeared to be flying out from the wall to which they were attached. Hanging straight over the bed, the new canopy was similar to a cantilever deck umbrella and was bedecked in point lace and ribbons. This model was such the rage that if you wanted yours made by the Bon brothers, the French bed designers of the moment, you had to wait a full year.

Whether it was a four-poster or a flying tester, canopy beds were valuable. If you were unlucky in cards, you could play another hand by putting your bed hangings up as stakes. In 1693, as a gift for completing a successful medical procedure, Louis XIV presented his surgeon, Monsieur Felix, with several such beds. Those gifts, however, paled in comparison to the one trimmed in velvet and silk embroidery that the king gave to the Swedish ambassador. There were 413 canopy beds in Versailles, so gifting a few here or there wouldn't have made much of a dent in Louis's collection.

"Never believe a man who says he doesn't like a canopy bed."

—MARIO BUATTA, AMERICAN DESIGNER

Through hundreds of years, canopy beds have remained en vogue in one form or another. In the United States during the 1950s and '60s, they were mostly found in country inns and little girls' bedrooms. In 1984, they rose to an uber-trend after American design legend Mario Buatta used one in a bedroom at the annual Kips Bay Decorator Show House in New York City. Buatta's version was a flat canopy attached to the ceiling, hung with frothy white curtains that were trimmed with yards of bobble fringe. *Architectural Digest* called it "the bedroom that shook the world."

Canopy Bed

Cornice with Acanthus **1.**

Cornice Frame **2**

Cantoon Armature **3**

Cantoon **4**

Spacer **5**

Tester Frame **6**

Tester **7**

Upper Valance **8**

Inner Valance **9**

Festoon Drape **10**

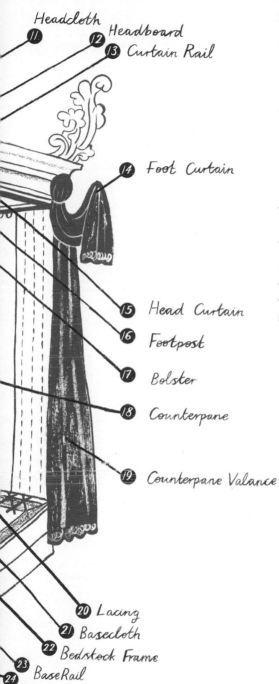

Headcloth
11

Headboard
12

Curtain Rail
13

Foot Curtain
14

Head Curtain
15

Footpost
16

Bolster
17

Counterpane
18

Counterpane Valance
19

Lacing
20

Basecloth
21

Bedstock Frame
22

BaseRail
23

Base Valance
24

After his success at Kips Bay, Buatta designed bedrooms for an impressive roster of moguls, socialites, and celebrities, including Billy Joel and Mariah Carey. After creating an over-the-top feminine canopy for a home in New Jersey, the designer called the homeowners to see how they liked it. He managed to get a hold of their maid, who reported, "I take the meals upstairs on a tray and they don't open the door." It turns out the couple got into the bed on Friday night and didn't get out all weekend.

If that's not endorsement enough, consider that on the days you have no energy to make your bed, you can simply snap the curtains shut.

Chaise Longue

The chaise longue is extravagant in its impracticality. No one *needs* a piece of furniture that looks like a stretched-out armchair. The French name simply means "long chair," and almost everyone pronounces it the wrong way. Most of us say chaise (shayz) correctly, but longue is where the linguistic rubber meets the road. It's *lawng*, not lounge. In fact, language usage expert Bryan A. Garner calls saying or writing "chaise lounge" an "embarrassing error" and distinctly "low-rent." Ouch. So unless your French is on point, just call it a *chaise*.

Its lineage can be traced back to ancient Egyptians, who originated the blend of a chair and a daybed. The chaise was the perfect seat for a languid midafternoon respite from the desert sun (often while being fanned by a servant). The Greeks, and later the Romans, put the piece to work in their homes and used it for sitting (or rather, reclining) at the table. The wooden chaise was made comfortable with pillows, loose covers, and the pelts of exotic animals like zebras and leopards. But when dining while lying down fell out of favor during the Middle Ages (too much a reminder of the self-indulgent Romans), the chaise was retired as well.

That is, until the eighteenth century, when lounging, which spread from France through all of Europe, became the preferred way to while away an afternoon (Marie-Antoinette style with champagne coupe in hand). The chaise was perfectly suited for the task. Unlike the Roman version, which was the purview of the masculine diner, this time it was a feature of a lady's boudoir.

At the start of the nineteenth century, the chaise had its shining moment. The famous French painter Jacques-Louis David painted the alluringly beautiful twenty-three-year-old socialite Madame Récamier seductively reclining on one, her feet bare. The portrayal shocked even the louche Parisians; at the time, women were expected to cover their naked feet with a small embroidered silk throw when receiving guests. The portrait was a marketing coup for the chaise that would have made Madison Avenue proud. Even in 1800, sex sold.

The Victorians moved the chaise longue out of the boudoir and into their over-furnished living rooms. It stood ready to catch a lady who was dizzy and short of breath as a consequence of her too-tight corset (thus giving it the name the "fainting couch").

It also became a core element of late-nineteenth-century Freudian psychoanalysis. Early in his career, Sigmund Freud used hypnosis to treat his clients. He found that they were more relaxed, open, and receptive to suggestions when they lay down, facing away from him. Though Freud eventually abandoned hypnosis as a technique, he continued to use the chaise when treating patients. In fact, a chaise covered in a red Turkish carpet took center stage in his London office.

In the 1930s, the chaise longue moved from the psychoanalyst's office to the silver screen. Any leading lady worth her salt—Greta Garbo, Jean Harlow, Gloria Swanson—draped herself seductively across one for photos and film shoots, generally clothed in a low-cut, spaghetti-strap satin nightgown. Today, it remains a staple of photo shoots for movie stars, fashion

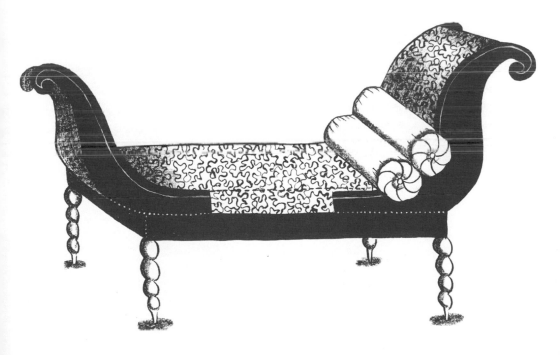

models, and even the occasional business executive looking to infuse femininity into her image.

> ## "If a visitor is announced, you are to receive him in a standing position—never lying on the chaise longue."

—KONSTANZE VON FRANKEN,
HANDBOOK OF GOOD FORM & FINE
MANNERS, *BERLIN, 1922*

In 1986, inspired by Madame Récamier's portrait, Australian designer Marc Newson created the Lockheed Lounge to emulate a "globule of mercury." (Possibly he found her languid posture resembled the liquid element.) He covered a foam prototype with sheets of pounded aluminum held together with rivets, giving the piece the look of a Lockheed plane. It was sold at auction in 2015 for $3.7 million, breaking all sales records for a single work by a living designer. (It certainly didn't hurt marketing efforts that Madonna had featured it in her 1993 music video for "Rain.")

Today's fast-paced lifestyle doesn't allow much time for lounging, and for the most part, the stand-alone chaise longue has been replaced by sofas and chairs in our public and private living spaces. But if you have the space, you can find a sectional with a chaise add-on that just might be enough to tempt you into slowing down.

Champagne Coupe

In the modern era, a tall, slim, elegant flute is the glass of choice for sipping champagne. But when the French first began to drink the effervescent wine, neither the drink nor the vessel was quite so refined.

In its earliest iterations in the seventeenth century, champagne wasn't so much a beverage to be savored as a drink to be slammed back like a shot of tequila. The sparkling wines had a lot of sediment, or dregs (an issue that wasn't resolved until the nineteenth century), so it was poured into round, saucer-shaped glass bowls on a stem, then downed in one gulp. Once finished, drinkers would turn their glasses over in a waste bowl to allow the sediment to drain out before the glass was refilled.

Legend has it that the first champagne coupe was formed in the shape of a woman's breast. Some say the breast in question belonged to Helen of Troy. Other conjectured muses were Marie-Antoinette or Madame de Pompadour, mistress of Louis XV of France. The inspiration isn't as far-fetched as it may sound: The ancient Greeks drank out of breast-shaped vessels called *mastos* (Greek for "breast"), complete with an articulated nipple.

While it's unlikely that anyone actually lent their breast as a cup mold, the fact that the rumor persists says something about the perceived sexiness of the coupe. And indeed, the champagne coupe has long been associated with sex: Prospective dancers for the celebrated nineteenth-century Belle Époque cabaret Folies Bergère were subject to a "champagne glass test," where their naked breast had to fit perfectly into a glass before they were given the job. The coupe was the glass of choice for free-spirited 1920s flappers, and both Marilyn Monroe and Sophia Loren were photographed imbibing from coupes. But it can also be elegant, as Jackie Kennedy demonstrated when she sipped bubbly from one at the Stork Club in Manhattan during John F. Kennedy's thirty-ninth birthday celebration. And for a party

WHAT IS CHAMPAGNE?

• • • • • • • • • • •

Before the seventeenth century, still wine was preferred over bubbly. The challenge? All wines start to fizz the moment the wine is pressed, when the yeast on the grape skins comes into contact with the sugar in the grape juice. Believe it or not, Dom Pérignon, who is frequently credited with inventing champagne in the 1690s, actually worked tirelessly to eliminate those embarrassing bubbles from his wines. (His knowledge of how to control the bubbles came in handy when makers began to try to render their spirits effervescent.) And while today true champagne can only officially be produced in the Champagne region of France, the drink as we know it now was actually born in the Limoux area of Languedoc. (Champagne just did a better marketing job.).

By the time Louis XV deemed champagne his favorite drink, Europeans had just begun to appreciate it (a dual result of winemakers learning how to harness the bubbles and contemporary doctors touting supposed health benefits, like increased virility and gout prevention). But only a few producers were able to master the art of making it, which was as dangerous as it was demanding. The wine was so unpredictable that, in an effort to prevent injury from a spontaneously bursting bottle, cellar workers were outfitted with heavy iron masks, like those of a baseball catcher. "I know one cellar in which there are three men who have each lost an eye," wrote nineteenth-century wine trader Thomas George Shaw. Of course, the difficulty of production only made champagne more expensive—and therefore more desirable for those who could afford it.

trick, from the 1930s through the 1960s, a favorite way to serve champagne was to create a pyramid of coupes and then pour the bubbly in the top glass, letting it cascade down and fill all the glasses in the tower.

The breast-shaped champagne vessel also has its share of modern iterations. In 1988, Morris Wilkins was granted Patent No. D294290, a design for a coupe-shaped hot tub that became a symbol for hotels like Cove Haven Resorts, a certain kind of honeymoon destination in the Pocono Mountains of Pennsylvania. In 2008, the designer Karl Lagerfeld created a breast-inspired bowl for Dom Pérignon that was a tribute to model Claudia Schiffer's twenty-five years in the fashion industry. And in 2014, model Kate Moss lent her left breast to be used as the prototype for a coupe commissioned by London's 34 Restaurant.

"I had taken two finger-bowls of champagne, and the scene had changed before my eyes into something significant, elemental, and profound."

—NICK (DRINKING FROM A CHAMPAGNE COUPE, OF COURSE) IN THE GREAT GATSBY BY F. SCOTT FITZGERALD

By the 1980s and '90s, wine aficionados turned their noses up at champagne served in a coupe, claiming that an elongated flute prolonged the trademark bubbles and enhanced both the taste and the aroma of the wine. But if you're willing to sacrifice a few bubbles for a lot of style, the coupe is a classic choice. After all, if you have to worry about your bubbles disappearing too quickly, maybe you're just not drinking fast enough.

ENTHUSIASTIC ENDORSERS

....

From Winston Churchill to Napoleon Bonaparte to Mark Twain, everyone who was anyone seemed to have something to say about champagne.

"In victory, you deserve champagne; in defeat, you need it," Churchill is recorded as saying in 1946. He was speaking to Madame Odette Pol Roger, the maker of his favorite brand of champagne. The two were great friends. Madame sent him the 1928 Pol Roger every year on his birthday, from their meeting in 1944 until the vintage ran out in 1953. After that, he received a bottle of the 1934 vintage until his death in 1965.

Madame de Pompadour, Louis XV's mistress, once observed, "Champagne is the only drink that leaves a woman still beautiful after drinking it." And she should know: She was one of Claude Moët's (of Moët & Chandon fame) most loyal customers.

Chess Set

Chess is one of the oldest board games to have survived to the present day. Our modern version is directly descended from a Hindu game called *chaturanga* (the Sanskrit term for four limbs and also the name of that push-up yoga pose). Developed in 500 c.e., it was played by four opponents. Each player would cast dice to determine the movement of each of the pieces (all male figures). Eventually, the game lost two players and the dice, making it a challenge of intellect rather than luck. In that form, it spread from India to Persia. When the Arabs conquered Persia in the seventh century, they discovered and fell in love with the game; a century later, they brought chess with them when they invaded southern Europe.

The queen piece joined the chessmen in medieval Europe. By 1200, the piece was included in sets all over Europe. Perhaps one of the reasons that the queen was so welcome on the board of the game of kings was that real-life royal women so often played it. A chess set was the on-trend wedding gift for a medieval princess bride-to-be. It was also a fixture in a wealthy medieval home; knowing how to play chess (along with reading, playing an instrument, and dancing) was an indication of status and good breeding. It didn't hurt that chess provided an excuse to meet with members of the opposite sex in the privacy of a boudoir or garden.

Women found chess useful post-marriage, too. In 1194, the Sicilian princess Constance Hauteville gave birth at age forty-one to her first and only child, the future emperor Frederick II. Unlike most royal women, who gave their baby over to wet nurses, Constance nursed the princeling herself. She passed the long hours in bed by playing chess with her ladies-in-waiting. Other aristocratic women followed suit, and soon chess sets were marketed specifically to new mothers.

Prior to 1849, there wasn't a standard accepted form for chess pieces; each was unique to an individual set. This was fine if you were familiar with the pieces and just playing a friendly game. But in competition, the last thing you wanted to

'Staunton Chess Set'

Pawn

Queen

Knight

Bishop

Rook

King

focus on was discerning the rook from the pawn. By the mid-nineteenth century, posh chess clubs were a fixture of English society. Their members refused to play with another player's set. It was a sort of men's club mutiny that just wouldn't do.

Enter Nathaniel Cooke, editor at the *Illustrated London News*, where chess master Howard Staunton was a columnist. (Staunton organized the first international chess tournament in 1851.) Together, the men designed a chess set with figures based on neoclassical design elements and named it after Staunton. (This wasn't entirely altruistic on Cooke's part; his brother-in-law owned a company, Jaques of London, that produced and sold games like croquet and table tennis.) Staunton's design is the one most people recognize today. It has since become the accepted version at tournaments according to the international rules of chess.

While the Staunton set might be the standard on the competition circuit, the desire for unique chess sets hasn't abated. In 1973, former Beatle Ringo Starr commissioned British silversmiths at luxury good purveyor Asprey to create gold and sterling silver pieces modeled from castings of his ringed fingers. The bishop is represented by fingers bestowing a blessing, and a fist stands in for the castle. For those who'd like something equally special but a little less narcissistic, designer Jonathan Adler channeled the Halston-era 1970s with a Lucite design sold in his eponymous boutiques.

Today, chess sets come in all kinds of materials: gold, silver, bronze, ivory, amber, jade, onyx, lapis, marble, wood, glass, plastic, and porcelain. It's also one of the few game boards that doesn't get returned to the box; instead, it's often given pride of place on a coffee table, desk, or bookshelf. You can't really say the same of Monopoly.

Chiavari Chair

From wedding receptions to the Golden Globes to dinners at the White House, if it's a sophisticated event, chances are you'll be sitting in a Chiavari chair. This light, easily stackable, and graceful piece of furniture is a favorite when it's time to find a seat at a party.

The Chiavari is a marriage of French elegance and Italian élan. In 1807, Marquis Stefano Rivarola of Chiavari, Italy, was visiting Paris, where he spotted a new style of chair that was all the rage: the Louis XV panel-back chair. As president of the Economic Society of Chiavari, Rivarola was convinced that the chair could be made better in his hometown. He returned to his palazzo on the Italian Riviera with Parisian samples in hand and marched them to the town's best woodworker, Giuseppe Gaetano Descalzi. When Descalzi saw the Parisian samples, he knew just what to do. He stripped off all the upholstery, which instantly created a more streamlined design. Then, he slimmed down the wooden frame so that the back and legs were narrower, and finally, straightened the curved

cabriole legs. His changes resulted in a chair that was lighter than the Parisian version and more sophisticated in its simplicity. In honor of its place of origin, he dubbed his creation *Chiavarine*, or little Chiavari.

If you've ever tried to carry a heavy oak chair from one room to another, you'll understand why the elegant Chiavari was an instant hit. Most chairs of the time were hefty and ornately carved. They were intended to remain in situ (and threw your back out if you tried to prove otherwise). Chairs were often so substantial that they required a servant to pull it back, just so you could take your seat.

Everyone who was anyone had a Chiavari. Queen Victoria famously sat in a Chiavari-style chair when she shaped European policy at her beloved Osborne House on the Isle of Wight. Crown Prince Friedrich of Prussia used them when he remodeled Charlottenhof Palace in Potsdam. Napoleon III and his fashion-forward wife, Eugénie, had Chiavari chairs at both their Château de Saint-Cloud and Fontainebleau residences.

CHIAVARI CHAIR

The best way to promote a successful product is to stick it in the hands of a celebrity. And leave it to royalty—American and European—to make something chic. On September 12, 1953, after three hours greeting guests in her wedding receiving line, Jackie Kennedy finally got to sit down. She, her new husband John F. Kennedy, and their 1,300 wedding guests were seated in Chiavari chairs to eat a wedding luncheon of pineapple cups, chicken à la king, and sliced ham and potatoes. Three years later, when, at her wedding reception, Grace Kelly sat next to her new husband, Prince Rainier of Monaco, in a Chiavari, the deal was sealed: The Chiavari became the official seat of choice at weddings, forever after supplanting the metal folding chair.

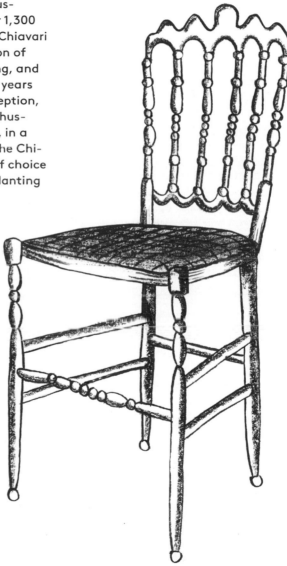

Chopsticks

Chopsticks were first used 5,000 years ago in China, which means that they predate forks by about 3,500 years. The tool was the perfect implement for the Chinese way of cooking and eating. Unlike in Western culture, where meat was eaten in large pieces and required knives to consume, most people in China served meat as a condiment, not the main ingredient. Housewives purchased the precut meat from butchers, who used a fierce-looking implement called a *tous* to butcher the meat. The small pieces of thin-sliced or chopped animal protein and larger quantities of vegetables were cooked quickly over a hot fire. It wasn't just practical; there was also an element of the spiritual. The Chinese people revered the philosopher Confucius, who wrote, "The honorable and upright man keeps well away from both the slaughterhouse and the kitchen. And he allows no knives on his table."

While the poor made do with implements crafted of wood or bamboo, the rich used chopsticks made from expensive materials like ivory, jade, lacquer, and even silver. In fact, the silver chopsticks used by the emperors and their families were considered a necessity, not a luxury. They were needed to keep the family safe. It was believed that silver would turn black if it touched arsenic. (It does not. However, silver *does* discolor on contact with certain ingredients, like rotten eggs, onion, and garlic, which release hydrogen sulfide.)

By 500 C.E., chopsticks were used in Japan, Vietnam, and Korea. Their spread followed food trends: first as

QUICK STICKS

....

But why do we call these two sticks that don't do any chopping "chopsticks"? The word is derived from the Chinese Pidgin English phrase "chop chop," meaning to hurry up. The translation for the Chinese word is kuàizi (筷子), *which literally means "quick stick." It was harder to say, so "chop" was combined with the English word "stick." And once you master them, you'll find that chopsticks are quick sticks indeed.*

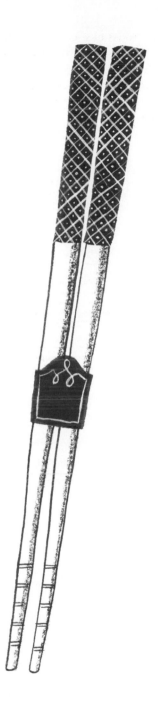

wheat-flour foods like noodles and dumplings were more widely consumed throughout Asia, and then as rice became the predominant food in the eleventh century.

Each culture adapted them to fit within the spheres of their own eating rituals. Japanese chopsticks, for instance, are shorter than the Chinese version; their length enables the diner to hold a bento box in one hand while using the implements to get into the box's tiny compartments. Korean chopsticks are often made of stainless steel with ridges on the edges that grip slippery foods more easily. (Unlike the Chinese and Japanese, Koreans eat their rice with a spoon.) Today, chopsticks are used by more than one-fifth of the world's population.

Chopsticks, which must be used in pairs, are also imbued with matrimonial symbolism. In Guizhou, China, a mother will take red paper–wrapped chopsticks to a girl's family to propose marriage on behalf of her lovestruck son. In the coastal regions north of Shanghai, chopsticks are a favorite wedding favor given by the groom. In Henan, a central province considered to be the cradle of Chinese civilization, guests "steal" the chopsticks at the wedding banquet to partake in the good fortune of the newlyweds.

In the West, we are most familiar with *waribashi*, disposable chopsticks made from cheap wood. Though they might seem like the Asian equivalent to paper plates and cups, they aren't a modern invention. Waribashi were used in the first Japanese restaurants in the eighteenth century. There is a Shinto belief that something that has been in another's mouth picks up aspects of their personality; therefore, you did not share chopsticks, even if they had been washed. Restaurateurs wanted to ensure that customers had unsullied utensils, and thus disposable chopsticks were born. The breaking apart of waribashi is still the sign that a meal is about to commence.

Japanese Chopsticks Faux Pas

1. Never let a liquid drip like tears from the end of the chopstick (crying chopsticks, namida-bashi).

2. Don't allow your chopsticks to hover over dishes (hesitating chopsticks, mayoi-bashi).

3. Don't use your chopsticks as a spoon (scooping chopsticks, yoko-bashi).

4. Never use your chopsticks like a knife (piercing chopsticks, sashi-bashi).

5. Don't lick off fragments from the end of your chopsticks (licked chopsticks, neburi-bashi).

Clock

Our preoccupation with keeping track of time dates back thousands of years. Before 1300 B.C.E, the Egyptians divided the day into twenty-four hours, measuring the passing daylight hours with a shadow clock, or sundial; the night hours were measured by the rising of certain stars or by the slow drip of water out of a marked bowl.

Almost ten centuries later, the Greek philosopher Plato devised a water-powered clock that whistled like a teakettle to wake his students for their 4 a.m. study. The downside was that Plato had to fill the clock with water six hours ahead of time, so he wasn't getting much sleep either. A version of the water clock was used in both Greek and Roman courts to make sure that speakers kept within their allotted time. To stop the clock, the water hole was blocked with wax, which could be removed and the clock restarted. Though it was his own invention, Plato lamented that lawyers were "driven by the water clock . . . never at leisure." Some things never change.

If Plato thought his fellow citizens were slaves to a schedule, he would have been appalled by the time-obsessed Chinese. Their primary motivation was dynastic: Court astrologers had to keep track of the precise time of conception of the emperor's many children because the heir to the throne was selected by horoscope and cosmological readings. In an attempt to improve accuracy, the Chinese modified the water clock with the use of mercury. It was still not quite precise enough, and in 723 C.E., a mathematically savvy Buddhist monk developed the first mechanical clock. It was more accurate than the mercury version but the gears were water-powered, and after only a few years the bronze and iron mechanisms corroded. Foiled again.

While Chinese clock technology became more complex and sophisticated, timekeeping in Europe was still relatively primitive. In ninth-century England, King Alfred the Great commissioned candles embedded with bells. Each hour, as the candle

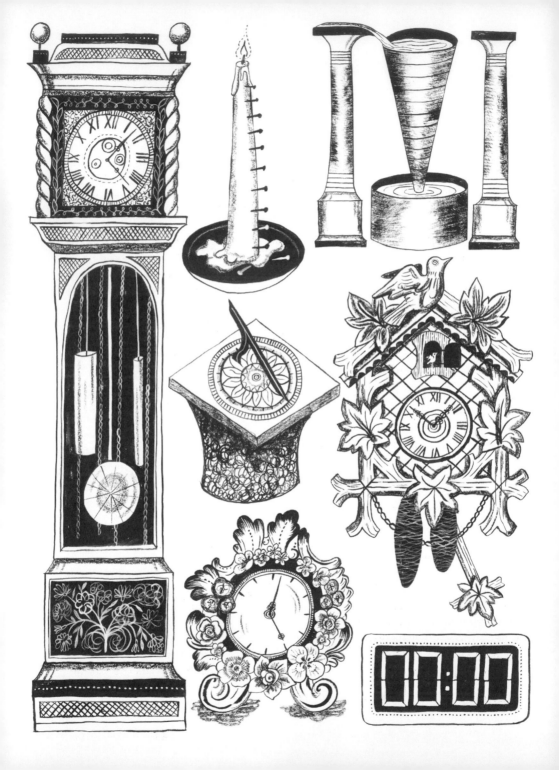

TIME OUT(SIDE)

....

Thomas Jefferson designed a grand clock for the entryway of his Virginia home, Monticello. In addition to displaying the hour, the clock told the days of the week by the slow descent of cannonballs along a device that ran from the ceiling to the floor. It had a duplicate face on the façade of the home, so that those strolling in the garden could glance back at the house for a time check.

The move from public object to private luxury was a slow one. The first domestic clocks had to be rather large to accommodate the swinging arc of the pendulum, which, in early clocks, was more accurate than gears. Initially, only wealthy aristocrats and royalty would have had clocks in their homes—and that was more from a desire to possess the latest gadget than for a real need to mark time. But by the eighteenth century, clockmakers had figured out how to reduce the size of the pendulum, and timepieces became a common household item.

melted, a bell would drop with a ping into a metal dish. For most Europeans, though, keeping time was of little concern; they rose with the sun and went to bed shortly after night fell. But in monasteries, where prayer ordered the day, marking time was more important. Monks drove the market for clocks—and, in some cases, made them.

As the population grew, settlements became towns and towns grew into cities. By the middle of the fourteenth century, most European cities had cathedral towers with clocks that chimed the hour, letting people know when to go to church and when to begin and end work. By the sixteenth century, the concept of marking time had become so important that city dwellers led their life by the clock, even relying on night watchmen, who cried out the time every hour on the hour.

> "A wizard is never late, nor is he early, he arrives precisely when he means to."

—*GANDALF*, THE FELLOWSHIP OF THE RING *BY J.R.R. TOLKIEN*

Clocks designed and manufactured in France became all the rage. These *objets* were over-the-top: elaborate with porcelain flowers for a lady's bedroom or gilt bronze for the mantle. There were sixty-six clocks in Napoleon's chateau, Fontainebleau—which

43

sounds extravagant until you realize the palace had 1,500 rooms. (Even emperors had a bottom line.) The only room in the house that never had a clock? The dining room, so as not to interfere with the leisurely pace of the meal. How civilized!

It wasn't until the Industrial Revolution that telling time became a necessity for daily life. Many factory workers couldn't afford a clock, so they paid a "knocker-upper" a penny a month to make sure they woke on time. Armed with a lantern, cane, and watch, knocker-uppers walked the streets, tapping on the windowpanes of their clients to rouse them for work.

As the nineteenth century progressed, private time became as regulated as public time. Good housekeeping became synonymous with precise timekeeping. In her *Book of Household Management*, Mrs. Beeton observed, "A good clock in the kitchen is an essential, and punctuality and strict observance of time with regard to everything . . . should be insisted upon." There were set times for meals, and if the house was particularly pious, there might also be a set time for prayer. An unintentionally late dinner was a social disaster for the mistress of the household, and to arrive late was equally calamitous. "The besetting fear of my debutante self," remembered Lady Cynthia Asquith, who had been presented at court in 1907, "is that I should be late for dinner."

PLAYING FOR TIME

• • • • • • • • • • • •

The Chinese Cosmic Engine, built by the astronomer Su Song in the eleventh century, was a 30-foot [9.1-m] tower built for observing the stars. It was an ancestor of the great public mechanical clocks of Europe—and, eventually, the cuckoo clock. At the base of the tower was a five-floor pagoda-like structure. Each floor had its own doorway, through which wooden puppets appeared at regular intervals, playing musical instruments to announce the changing time. The tower was powered by an enormous waterwheel. Scoops at the end of the blades dripped water, causing the machinery to advance by one scoop every hour. The great clock ran uninterrupted for thirty-six years.

Cocktail Shaker

The cocktail shaker is not just the iconic symbol of a cocktail party; it also provides the soundtrack. Each clink of ice accompanies an escalation in the festivities. It's the sound of author Dashiell Hammett's Nick and Nora Charles, who shook to the tempo of foxtrots for their Manhattans, with a two-step for a dry martini. It brings to mind James Bond and his beverage of choice: a "very strong and very cold and very well-made" Vesper martini, named for Bond girl Vesper Lynd. (Three measures gin, one measure vodka, and one-half measure Kina Lillet, shaken, not stirred.) It's the accompaniment to the indulgent three-martini lunch, epitomized by television's most famous ad executives, Don Draper and Roger Sterling.

In the 1800s, American bartenders mixed drinks by pouring the ice—a new luxury introduced thanks to the advent of refrigerated transportation—and alcohol back and forth between tumblers. The flashier the bartender's display, the better. (Think Tom Cruise in the 1988 film *Cocktail*.) *New York Tribune* reporter George Foster was impressed; in 1848, he wrote of a bartender: "With his shirt sleeves rolled up and his face in a fiery glow, [he] seems to be pulling long ribbons of julep out of a tin cup." That tin cup was the forerunner of the cocktail shaker we know today.

> **"Shake the shaker as hard as you can: don't just rock it: you are trying to wake it up, not send it to sleep."**
>
> —HENRY CRADDOCK, THE SAVOY COCKTAIL BOOK, *1930*

In the nineteenth century, many middle-class men spent their free time inventing and filing patents. Among them were numerous "improvements" on the two-cup design, including a device that agitated six two-piece shakers at the same time. There was the cocktail shaker with an air vent.

SHAKEN OR STIRRED?

. . . .

While James Bond may have preferred his Vesper shaken, not stirred, that's actually not the best preparation method. If your drink is made with only spirits, stirring is the way to go. Shaking foams things up, adding an undesirable texture to your should-be-smooth martini. It also affects the flavor profile. Banging all that ice around dilutes the drink and takes away some of its sweetness. This is fine if you're talking about an uber-sweet drink, like a daiquiri, but not so much for a martini. Sorry, Mr. Bond.

And there was a bell-shaped shaker; the mixologist used the handle of the bell to agitate the tumbler. None of these new versions really took hold until Brooklyn resident Edward Hauck created the three-piece shaker—a cup, lid, and strainer—in 1884. Whether it was the concept or the timing, Hauck's shaker was adopted by bartenders throughout the country.

Rather ironically, the arrival of Prohibition in the 1920s caused sales of Hauck's invention to skyrocket. Cocktail consumption was at an all-time high as amateur mixologists sought to render homemade bathtub gin more palatable. In the Art Deco–obsessed 1930s, as Zeppelins and skyscrapers reached for the skies, aerodynamically shaped silver mixers became a must-have item for the home. They were also a Hollywood favorite, both on- and off-screen. With the introduction of talking pictures in 1927, audiences could now hear the music of the rattling ice as the bartender made cocktail magic on-screen. Actress Marion Davies, girlfriend of newspaper tycoon William Randolph Hearst, loved a mixed drink. Gossip was that when Davies went for a swim in her 110-foot [33.5-m] foot saltwater pool at her Santa Monica mansion, she would sip from a series of cocktail shakers lined up along the pool's edge. Her behavior was extravagant even by Hollywood standards.

At the same time, in Washington, D.C., senators and congressmen found the intricacies of politics easier to navigate with a drink in hand. Franklin Delano Roosevelt (who was instrumental in repealing Prohibition in 1933) even brought his favorite cocktail set—a silver shaker with a bamboo motif and six matching cups in a blue velvet–lined, maroon leather case—to a Tehran summit in 1943 to talk war strategy with Winston Churchill and Joseph Stalin. There, Roosevelt reportedly served Stalin his first-ever dirty martini. The event prompted a Roosevelt official to describe those years as the "four martinis and let's have an agreement" era. Unfortunately for the rest of America, the shaker was in short supply during World War II. Companies that once made them now made artillery shells.

But postwar, cocktail culture exploded both in and out of the rec room. At the hard-drinking, fast-living Rat Pack parties held by Frank Sinatra, Dean Martin, and Sammy Davis Jr., the dress code was black tie with sunglasses, and a shaken martini was the epitome of cool. In the 1960s, the Madison Avenue crowd (calling Don Draper!) kept bartenders busy with three-martini lunches and cocktails after work.

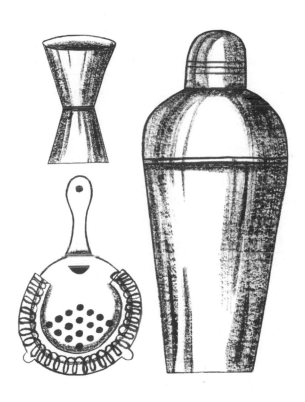

Crystal Chandelier

Chandeliers bring a little bit of glamour and fanciful magic into our everyday lives. The first generation of chandeliers was forged in the eleventh century in Constantinople (modern-day Istanbul), the center of the Byzantine Empire. There, artisans designed ornate circular holders for cups of clean-burning oil and hung them from the ceilings of mosques.

At that time in Europe, churches were lit by crude, cross-shaped contraptions outfitted with metal spikes that held tallow candles in place. These candles—*chandelles* in French—gave the fixture its name: The holder became known as the *chandelier*. These early European prototypes were so messy and unpleasant that the sixteenth-century French expression for extreme filth was a phrase that translates to "like a wooden chandelier."

When the European Crusaders returned from the religious wars in the Middle East in the twelfth century, they brought with them the more refined lighting fixture they had seen in mosques. Over the next five hundred years, European chandeliers slowly evolved into massive, crown-shaped iron devices that adorned churches, manors, and the great halls of castles. Then in the fifteenth century, designers

LUXE LIGHTING

• • • • • • • • • • • •

When Renaissance soldier and consummate entertainer Ippolito de' Medici held a party to celebrate the completion of his magnificent home, the Palazzo San Francesco, he didn't have quite enough chandeliers to make the statement he wanted—so he borrowed fourteen more from friends. It took three carpenters an entire day to hang them, and another four to create gilded paper decorations to be hung from the chandelier branches (each was painted with the coat of arms of all the principal guests). For added drama, Ippolito had the candles painted in his colors: dark red and orange.

in the city of Dinant (in modern-day Belgium) created a new model: Candles were held aloft by elegantly curving branches centered around a large brass sphere that reflected the flames. You can see one hiding behind the figures in Renaissance painter Jan van Eyck's masterpiece, the *Arnolfini Portrait*.

Around the time that brass chandeliers were making their way into all the fashionable homes of fifteenth- and sixteenth-century Europe, gem cutters in Milan, Italy, began crafting clear quartz into crystal forms. (The word "crystal" comes from the Greek *krystallos*, meaning "ice," because the ancient Greeks believed clear quartz was ice that was so frozen it could not melt.) Although quartz was difficult to work with, its complete transparency was more desirable than the smoky gray glass of the time. To incorporate quartz into chandeliers, the wire cage surrounding the candle branches of a chandelier was strung with small beads—creating a sort of pavé diamond effect—and then hung with sparkling pendants that appeared to be dripping off the frame. These dazzling chandeliers were the epitome of luxury and adorned the palaces of the Medicis in Florence, King Louis of France, and the kings of England.

In 1674, London glass merchant George Ravenscroft patented a new kind of glass called lead crystal, so named because it contained lead oxide. Even more brilliant and transparent than other glass of the time, it was also

SETTING THE MOOD

• • • • • • • • • • • •

If you've ever been at a bar when the lights come up at closing time, you know how quickly bad lighting can kill even the most romantic of moods. That was a chance Cleopatra was not willing to take when she set out to seduce Marc Antony. She had the flowers, the scent, the food, and the decor—but the real showstopper was the lighting. According to Greek biographer Plutarch, when Marc Antony arrived at the dinner, "he found the preparations to receive him magnificent beyond expression, but nothing so admirable as the great number of lights; for on a sudden there was let down altogether so great a number of branches with lights in them . . . some in squares, and some in circles, that the whole thing was a spectacle that has seldom been equaled for beauty." Shakespeare was so in awe of Plutarch's description that he lifted it—word for word—to set the mood for his play, Antony and Cleopatra.

slightly softer than rock crystal. This made it easier to cut the glass into decorative shapes with more facets—the better to reflect light. The Hall of Mirrors in Versailles is filled with early examples of lead crystal chandeliers.

Chandeliers were costly to light because of the many, many candles, and only special occasions justified the expense. In 1779, when King George III visited the Duchess of Portland, the English artist Mrs. Delany observed, "Her Grace had the house lighted up in the most magnificent manner; the chandelier in the great hall had not lighted up before twenty years." This lack of use is likely the reason so many elaborate chandeliers have survived intact. (A plus for antique shoppers.)

The crystal chandelier most commonly seen today was born in 1892, when Bohemian glassmaker Daniel Swarovski invented a precision-cutting machine for glass. His namesake company quickly became known for its crystal-encrusted jewelry.

Timing is everything in love and luxury, and Swarovski's entrée into the world of interior decor coincided perfectly with the opening of the Metropolitan Opera's new home at Lincoln Center in New York City. On September 16, 1966, twenty-one Swarovski crystal chandeliers, designed to look like starbursts, were suspended in midair above the stage. Just before the curtain rose on Samuel Barber's *Antony and Cleopatra*, the chandeliers, suspended on motorized winches, ascended majestically to the ceiling so as not to obstruct audience's sight lines. The first standing ovation at the Met was not for the opera, the singers, or the composer, but for the chandeliers.

Curule Chair

Devised in the desert, the curule chair is the ultimate power seat. The ancient Egyptians carried a collapsible version into battle, made with a wooden, *X*-shaped frame and slung leather seat, so the commanding officer would have a lofty place from which to view the action.

> **"The chair is a very difficult object. Everyone who has ever tried to make one knows that."**
>
> —*LUDWIG MIES VAN DER ROHE*

Around the sixth century B.C.E., the Romans (never afraid to borrow a good idea) created their own version. It was more elaborate, with arms and inverted *U*-shaped legs to make it more stable, and crafted from luxurious materials like ivory and ebony. The chair quickly became a symbol of prestige. It was only used by those in authority, including consuls, government officials, and dictators. As a coronation chair, the curule was *the* number one choice. In 44 B.C.E., when Julius Caesar wanted a little something special to commemorate his newly declared power, he commissioned a gilded version. He was given permission by the Senate to use it anywhere except the theater, where only priests were afforded that privilege. (That he was assassinated that same year suggests the golden chair may have been a step too far for Rome.)

The fall of Rome didn't spell the end for the curule, however. Throughout the Middle Ages, the classic Roman form was embraced by the ultra-elite of Europe: popes, princes, and kings. In 777, Charlemagne, the first recognized emperor in Western Europe, trumped Caesar's gilded chair with one made of solid gold.

Canvas Stool

Curule

Barcelona Chair

THE CHAIR THAT MAKES THE DIRECTOR'S CUT

· · · · · · · · · · · ·

The folding canvas chair found on movie sets everywhere is a direct descendent of the curule. First pro-duced in 1892 by the Wisconsin-based Gold Medal Camp Furniture Company, the collapsible armchair was designed for campers and yachtsmen. In the 1920s, the Hollywood crowd discov-ered it, and soon it became a fixture on movie sets, perfect for stars waiting for their close-ups. Stenciling names on the back made it easy to ensure that the cast had a place to rest (or spot who wasn't where they were supposed to be). Publicity stills like the one of Marlene Dietrich lounging in a direc-tor's chair with cigarette in hand on the set of The Garden of Allah *gave Gold Medal's business a boost. The company, now located in Tennessee, still makes the ever-popular chairs. Buy one, and you can be the star of your own show.*

During the Renaissance, subtle changes to the Roman design enhanced the aesthetics (if not the comfort) of the curule: The bottom supports began to take on a wavy S-curve and the legs crossed beneath the seat rose to support the arms and back. It was still the kingly choice of seat: When Charles II of England was crowned in 1651, he sat on an imposing version that was painstakingly uphol-stered in purple velvet and studded with hundreds of gilt-head nails.

But furniture fashions change, even for royalty, and slowly the throne—far more ornate and imposing—replaced the curule as their preferred seat. Not the most comfortable of perches, curules were relegated to the purview of museums and antique dealers by the twentieth century. But good design is timeless. When Parisian antiques dealer Serge Roche began making his own furniture in the 1930s, he created a mirrored-leg version that would have impressed Caesar himself. It certainly knocked the socks off New York dec-orator and tastemaker Elsie de Wolfe. She featured Roche's furniture in her Fifth Avenue showroom. She also sent a pair of curule stools to the only royalty American audiences recognized: the Hollywood variety. Cinema heartthrob Gary Cooper found a spot for them in his Los Angeles home.

Around the same time as the Roche version, designer and architect Ludwig Mies van der Rohe received a commis-sion to design furniture for the Spanish

THE ELEMENTS OF A HOME

royal family. He wanted to create an "important chair, a very elegant chair," and his inspiration was the curule. His take on the classic had a tufted leather seat and curule-style curved legs. It was the centerpiece of the German pavilion at the Barcelona Exposition, a World's Fair held in Spain. Van der Rohe redesigned the piece again in 1950, using modern techniques that allowed the frame to be molded from a single piece of stainless steel. Architecture critic Ada Louise Huxtable ardently declared the chair "the Rolls Royce of furniture."

Today, the Mies version of the curule, known as the Barcelona chair, retails for $5,500. Expensive, yes—but a bargain when you consider its royal lineage. Whether you find yourself lusting after the traditional curule of the Caesars or a contemporary version, perhaps you can sit a little easier knowing you have a chair fit for a king.

Deck Chair

Weather-hardy and able to withstand a beating, deck chairs must also be portable—the better to move from deck to porch or from backyard to beach. Therefore, they have a license to be just a bit more daring than their indoor cousins.

Both backyard decks and the reclining chairs that go with them hearken back to the golden era of ocean liners. The easily movable deck chair was originally used on a passenger ship. With a light wooden frame and a canvas body, it collapsed perfectly flat, was stackable, and could be stored without taking up too much space. On the British cruise line P&O, passengers would make a mad dash for unoccupied seats each morning. To solve the seating issue, passengers were encouraged to pack a deck chair of their own for the two-week journey across the Atlantic.

American John Cham patented the deck chair in 1855. The timing was ser-endipitous. In the nineteenth century, leisure travel, once the purview of the elite, was suddenly within reach of a growing middle class. Cham's orig-

inal deck chair was made with drab olive canvas, but the British improved on the design with a brightly colored striped material. The simple version that worked so well at sea seemed to the British equally appropriate for the sand—and quickly, the canvas chair became synonymous with summer pleasures. One could rent it by the hour at beaches or parks, and settle in to enjoy seaside fare of fish and chips or pink cotton candy.

In 1877, British inventor Joseph Fenby patented a new version of the deck chair made of a light wood. His version borrowed from the curule chair and folded together like a tent, rather than into a flat rectangle like the Cham model. Sold by sporting outfitter Abercrombie & Fitch, it was marketed as an officer or campaign chair, and it became an essential part of the outdoorsman's kit. In 1909, the ultimate outdoorsman, Teddy Roosevelt, was photographed in a Fenby chair while on safari in Tanzania.

The Fenby folding chair was the inspi-ration for three Argentinean architects:

Jorge Ferrari Hardoy, Antonio Bonet, and Juan Kurchan. In 1938, they collaborated on a foldable canvas seat that used tubular steel, rather than wood, for the frame. They called it the Butterfly Chair. Their design attracted the attention of the curator of industrial design at New York City's Museum of Modern Art, Edgar Kaufmann jr. (he insisted on using a lowercase *j* in jr.). Edgar's parents had just finished construction of their home, and he purchased two butterfly chairs as a gift for them. It so happens that the house was Fallingwater, one of the most iconic projects ever completed by Frank Lloyd Wright. (It's listed on *Smithsonian*'s "Life List of 28 Places to Visit Before You Die").

In 1947, the Knoll design firm acquired U.S. production rights for the Butterfly Chair; nearly five million were sold during the 1950s alone. But it is not a chair of yesteryear. Today it's both a dorm room staple and a museum collectible: You can view an original in the Museum of Modern Art's permanent collection.

The Butterfly Chair is not the only modern version of the deck chair. You can find the timeless design in outdoor patio furniture sets and collapsible beach chairs, interpreted in metal and plastic. Or you can spring for a high-end, classic version in teak and mahogany and feel like you're traveling first class through life.

ARRANGING DECK CHAIRS ON THE TITANIC

· · · · · · · · · · · ·

The Titanic *carried six hundred deck chairs made of beechwood; they featured slatted backs, woven rattan seats, and a hinged footrest that extended and transformed it into a chaise longue. The chairs were set out by the crewmen each morning, and then folded and tied with a rope in the evening. A few survived the ship's sinking. One of ten known existing chairs sold at auction in 2015 for about $150,000.*

Desk

For much of recorded history, thinking great thoughts was the province of the elite—but the actual writing was done by scribes. Even the most storied philosophers and orators of ancient Rome didn't put pen to paper (or stylus to tablet). Instead, they dictated their thoughts to a literate slave, whose "desk" was a box with a sloped top that could be placed on any flat surface. In the Middle Ages, that sloped surface was attached to legs for a more stable structure that made transcribing documents easier for monks.

With the dawn of the Age of Enlightenment in the eighteenth century and increased literacy, the physical act of writing became more mainstream. As people penned their own letters and documents, the desk started making its way into the home. The higher the status of the writer, the more finely crafted and elaborate the desk.

There were two types of desks available to the eighteenth-century writer (whether of letters, ledgers, or books). The *secretaire* (from *secretarius*, the Latin word for "writer") combined a writing surface with a set of drawers for storage. In a pre-password age, the best protection against would-be snoopers was a desk with hidden drawers and compartments, their existence known only to the furniture maker and the owner. The second desk option was a bureau: a flat writing table covered in leather or cloth, with few drawers. The secretaire allowed for more privacy, while the bureau displayed your papers for all to see.

There was a surprisingly large market for desks among eighteenth-century courtesans. It was critical to project the image of a "learned woman" to attract clients, and the writing desk became a key component of a well-appointed apartment. The most desirable model for courtesans was one veneered in an expensive wood, like tulipwood, and embellished with small porcelain plaques. The secretaire's locked and concealed compartments were also quite useful for a woman with some secrets to keep.

Most desks were designed for one user. But in the 1800s, the partners' desk became popular. Designed for senior banking officials, it was broad enough to accommodate two users, who faced each other across the desk. Constructed out of the best materials available, befitting the user's high social status, the body was often made of mahogany or walnut and the top fitted with a leather insert to provide a more resilient surface for writing. The desk was finished with shiny brass hardware and included a set of drawers and cabinets on either side of the piece.

At the end of the nineteenth century—an era of furniture innovation and whimsy—Stephen Hedges patented a space-saving desk that looked and functioned like a side table. The hinged desktop could be flipped back to reveal a chair beneath and a flat surface with a lockable drawer. It became

THE RESOLUTE DESK

· · · · · · · ·

Today, one of the most famous desks in the world sits in the Oval Office of the White House. The large partners' desk was made with wood from the Resolute, an abandoned British Arctic exploration ship that was recovered by an American whaler and returned to Queen Victoria. In gratitude, she had the desk made from the ship's English oak timbers and gifted it to President Rutherford B. Hayes. Every president since Hayes, except for Johnson, Nixon, and Ford, has used the desk either in the Oval Office or in the Residence.

The Resolute desk, as it is now known, has gone through many modifications. Initially it had an open kneehole front, but Franklin Roosevelt added a hinged front panel to hide his leg braces. John F. Kennedy's son, John Jr., called the desk "his house" and the panel "the secret door." The photo of young John Jr. peeking out from under the desk while his father reviewed papers hit newsstands in Look magazine days after the president's assassination. It made the desk a symbol of the Camelot myth of a youthful president running the country with a young family by his side.

known as the Aaron Burr desk after a *New York Herald* article claimed that Burr had penned his letter challenging Alexander Hamilton to a duel from one of them. The veracity of the story is suspect, but the name stuck.

The standing desk may feel like a modern invention, but it's been a work staple since the 1400s. Leonardo da Vinci is believed to have sketched his designs for flying machines and armored cars while standing. And in the late eighteenth century, some considered sitting to be a sign of slacking. "A sedentary life may be injurious," the Presbyterian minister Job Orton wrote in 1797. "It must therefore be your resolute care to keep your body as upright as possible when you read and write; never stoop your head nor bend your breast. To prevent this, you should get a standing desk."

The list of standing desk fans is certainly impressive. Thomas Jefferson designed his own standing desk with six legs for added stability and an adjustable slanted top large enough for an oversize book. His colleague, Senator Elijah Boardman, had a standing desk made with a built-in bookcase. Writers Charles Dickens and Ernest Hemingway both used standing desks. Hemingway fashioned his out of a waist-high bookcase. So if you stand in the place where you work, you're joining an impressive lineage.

Dollhouse

In 1557, a miniature version of a four-story palace was gifted to Albert V, the Duke of Bavaria. Albert had seven children, but this mini-castle—the earliest known dollhouse—wasn't intended for their grubby little fingers. This was not a child's toy, but a cabinet of curiosities made to delight the duke, a voracious collector of antiquities and art. From the miniature pewter dishes and rotisserie chicken roasting in the kitchen to the long table with silver legs in the ballroom, every tiny object was executed in exacting detail.

For the next hundred years, the trend of creating miniature worlds slowly gathered steam. At the time, worldly gentlemen would commission furniture to house their marvelous collections of nature and innovation. These cabinets of curiosity were a visual way to demonstrate the breadth of their knowledge (and the size of their pocketbooks).

Women had smaller-scale versions of the domestic spaces known as "baby houses," a reference to their size, not their audience. These miniature homes were exact copies of the owner's home.

Some women extended their reach beyond domestic spaces. The German princess Augusta Dorothea von Schwarzburg-Arnstadt spent decades re-creating her court, town, and the surrounding countryside in miniature. Called *Mon Plaisir*, the scaled-down village is filled with shops, houses, and townspeople, and it plunged the princess deeply in debt.

In addition to wowing dinner guests, baby houses were also used as teaching tools for young girls who needed to learn the art of housekeeping. In 1631, German Anna Köferlin had her woodcutter husband construct a 9-foot [2.7-m] dollhouse. She charged admission for the young to be educated in the art of domesticity.

For the next three hundred years, adults assembled elaborate, unique dollhouses. As our modern concept of childhood took hold in society, dollhouses became a popular toy for young girls. They were considered appropriately domestic, and encouraged quiet play. In the early 1800s, craftsmen began crafting dollhouses for toyshops, making buildings that represented nearly every kind of

A MIRACULOUS HOUSE

••••••••••

In 1705, after nine years of painstaking curation, Petronella Oortman, a wealthy Dutch widow, revealed her dollhouse to friends in her Amsterdam living room. It's because of this dollhouse that history has any record of Petronella at all. Like the most fashionable Dutch baby houses, Petronella's diminutive rooms were contained within a cabinet. Hers was made of tortoiseshell with pewter inlays. When the doors were closed, there was no hint of the magical wonderland contained within the cabinet.

Petronella and her guests would spend entire evenings marveling over the enchanting tableaus. The interior mirrored her nine-room home along one of Amsterdam's most exclusive canals—and cost just as much. Anything she owned in real life was reproduced to scale in the dollhouse so that her guests could see the mass of her wealth with just a single mesmerizing glance.

Each object was meticulously crafted by hand. The hallway mirrored the home's marble floor and the ceiling painting of Aurora, the goddess of dawn. The salon was decorated with floor-to-ceiling wall murals done by Dutch landscape painter Nicolaes Piemont, and featured eleven upholstered chairs, a backgammon table, and a tea table (with a top that folded down). Even the maid's room was accurate, with box beds, porcelain chamber pots, foot warmers, and a spinning wheel. The tiles were ceramic, the porcelain imported from China, and the flatware made of silver. The minute napkins and bed linens were monogrammed with Petronella's initials. This miraculous house was so enchanting that it became the inspiration for an international bestselling novel, The Miniaturist *by Jessie Burton, and is now part of the permanent collection of the Rijksmuseum in Amsterdam.*

dwelling, from single rooms in suburban tenements to luxurious townhouses. Soon, dollhouses and accessories, like almost all other consumer goods, were made in factories. Once miniatures were standardized and reproduced en masse thanks to the Industrial Revolution, collecting lost its challenge.

One notable exception was the dollhouse designed for Queen Mary by architect Sir Edwin Lutyens in the 1920s. Created to house and showcase miniature versions of the best work of thousands of Britain's finest artists, craftsmen, and manufacturers, the dollhouse became a national sensation. It was seen by 1.6 million visitors at the 1924 British Empire Exhibition. Today, it's still a highlight of a Windsor Castle tour. Crowds line up to gawk at the monogrammed linens, the shotguns that "break and load," and the garage of cars with engines that actually run.

Door, Knocker, and Knob

You probably don't give too much thought to your front door (unless you can't find your key). But this architectural feature is so weighted with cultural significance, symbolism, and ritual that it's hard to believe it stands upright at all. From the proper way to knock (not too forcefully, please!) to how you greet someone at the threshold, conventions and rules regarding doorway etiquette exist in abundance; after all, the front door separates the outside world from our private domestic spaces.

In medieval Europe, violent acts against the door and threshold of a house were considered more than simple acts of vandalism. It was an assault on the person, or persons, who lived there. In Germany, a blow to the door resulted in a more severe punishment than a blow to a person. And in the Holy Roman Empire, maliciously damaging a door (even without intruding) was considered a capital crime. That may seem harsh—but as the sole barrier between interior and exterior space in a time before alarm systems or locks, the door was considered sacred.

The Renaissance Italian architect Vincenzo Scamozzi advised making doors as attractive as possible. He suggested the door is to a house as a mouth is to a living creature. Some architects, like Federico Zuccari, took him literally. The front door Zuccari designed for the Palazzo Zuccari in 1592 resembles the oversize mouth of a grotesque stone monster, and is still a tourist attraction in Rome.

> **"The unstructured wall of a room is mute, but the door speaks."**
>
> —*GEORG SIMMEL, SOCIOLOGIST*

Like jewelry and accessories, hardware such as knockers, doorknobs, and locks can also enhance the appeal of an entrance. Knockers have been around almost as long as there have been doors. The ancient Greeks were the first to use them in the form of a heavy ring fastened to the door by a plate. The Romans followed suit—and as their empire spread, so did the knocker. It also became a symbolic item: Grabbing a door ring could signal the purchase of a property or the right to seize a home. A lion's head door ring announced a Christian lived there.

It's hard to know exactly when doorknobs became a standard fixture. Before (and if you were poor, during) the Middle Ages, most people drilled a hole in their front door and used a latchstring or piece of leather to open it. It was also at some point during this period that knocking with one hand became the custom (maybe due to New Testament images of Christ knocking); the Romans knocked on the door with their foot. Medieval blacksmiths forged the earliest doorknobs from iron. By the 1600s, whitesmiths, or tin workers, found that the malleable material could be used to create decorative versions. But these knobs did not turn: If your door had a doorknob, you still pushed or pulled the door open, and if you had a lock, you used the force of the key.

It wasn't until the late 1880s that doorknobs were fitted with sock-

STATEMENT DOORS

. . . .

For three years, speculation abounded in the elite enclave of Newport, Rhode Island. What were William K. Vanderbilt and his wife, Alva, building behind their 8-foot-[2.4-m-] high fence? The curious found out on August 19, 1892, when the fence came down and the doors of the Marble House were thrown open to welcome society's elite. The doors were marvels of engineering: 16 feet [4.9 m] high and 25 feet [7.6 m]wide, made of steel and glass, and each weighing more than a ton. For such impressive doors, you might expect some equally impressive doorknobs. You'd be wrong. The doors were knobless. Footmen dressed in maroon uniforms stood behind each door so guests would never need to exert themselves in order to open or close one.

ets and mechanisms that allowed them to turn the way that we're accustomed to today. In 1878, African American inventor Osbourn Dorsey took out patent #210,764 for a "door-holding device" compression-casting method that made it easier and faster to create brass or bronze doorknobs that were both uniform and ornamental. Now, designers and architects could create hardware that matched their aesthetic vision.

Door at the Palazzo Zuccari, Rome

In a world where first impressions count, decorative tweaks to a door can pack a significant punch. A coat of paint in a kicky color, or hardware with a unique finish or shape, can signal welcome even before the knock. Architect Claus Seligmann said the door was "the device that makes architecture possible." Without it, you merely have a box.

Knocking Through the Ages

Ancient Rome

Knock with the foot.

Middle Ages

Knock with a single hand (some in the Middle Ages preferred a more subtle touch and would cough to announce arrival).

Sixteenth-Century Cologne

In Cologne (modern-day Germany), important citizens brought servants with them to do the knocking.

Eighteenth-Century Versailles

No knocking allowed; instead, scratch the door with fingernails.

Duvet

Happiness guru Gretchen Rubin observed that making your bed each morning is one of the single best ways to boost your mood and set the tone for the rest of the day. If you've ever wrestled with straightening twisted sheets and smoothing wrinkled blankets while trying to get out the door on time, you might doubt her advice. Or perhaps you simply haven't considered the duvet. Essentially a comforter stuffed with feather, wool, or polyester and encased in a removable washable cover, the duvet eliminates the need for a top sheet and is the answer to every lazy bed maker's prayers.

It's not clear exactly when people realized that feathers might make for perfect blanket stuffing. We do know that feather blankets were used in Asia as early as the first century C.E. The covers were loosely quilted, with broad channels (pockets of stuffing created by stitching). This construction not only stopped feathers from ending up in one corner, but also allowed them to expand and hold in warm air. The downy soft feathers on the breast of the duck were the best for warmth, though it could take years to collect the 50 pounds [23 kg] needed for a featherbed.

In most of Europe and America, featherbeds were intended to be slept *on*. But by the seventeenth century, in the colder northern European countries like northern Germany and Scandinavia, people began sleeping under them as well. Featherbeds were valuable possessions and were usually included as a part of a dowry or an inheritance.

In 1700, English traveler Paul Rycaut tried to introduce this stuffed blanket to his countrymen by sending each of his friends 6 pounds [2.5 kg] of down with precise instructions on how to construct a blanket of their own. The newfangled bed cover obviously didn't catch on, because fifty years later, English author Thomas Nugent was completely baffled by the way featherbeds were used in northwestern Germany. "There is one thing very particular to them, that they do not cover themselves with bedclothes, but lay one feather-bed over, and another under," he wrote in his memoir, *The Grand Tour*.

It wasn't until the Victorian era that the forerunner to the duvet—the eiderdown—entered the British marketplace. Quilted and usually filled with cotton, silk, or synthetic fabrics (rarely with feathers), they were much heavier than a modern duvet and an effective substitute for heavy woolen blankets. Feather blankets may have been lighter, warmer, and more comfortable, but they were also attractive to vermin. At the time, most households were engaged in a constant battle against rodents and (horror of horrors!) bedbugs. And victory was elusive: In 1824, the stately bed in London's Mansion House (with its luxurious golden embroidered damask bed hangings) had to be burned after a close inspection revealed that a colony of creepy-crawlies had permanently moved into the feather stuffing. So it should be no surprise that medical professionals like Florence Nightingale advised the public to "never use a featherbed, either for the sick or well." But Victorians weren't minimalists, and found it difficult to resist the lure of downy softness. To achieve this without featherbeds, they typically layered multiple blankets and sheets similar to our modern setup: a top sheet, a couple of blankets, an eiderdown quilt, and a bedspread, depending on the season.

The duvet conquered the world of bedding about one hundred years later, thanks to the British interior designer Terence Conran. Traveling in the 1950s, the young Conran woke up in a Swedish bed covered by a down quilt encased in a cotton cover. (Encasing the down quilt in cotton seems to be a Swedish invention.) There was no top sheet or additional blankets in sight. The simplicity and casual chicness of the easy-to-make bed appealed to him. "I probably had a girl with me," Conran told the British newspaper the *Independent* in 2010. "And I thought that it was part of the mood at the time—liberated and sexy easy living." So in 1964, when Conran opened the first of his revolutionary design stores, Habitat, in London's Chelsea neighborhood, a key item was the duvet.

Habitat launched a persuasive campaign called the "ten-second bed." Demonstrators at stores throughout England spent their day making and unmaking beds to show customers just how quickly it could be done. Also appealing was the fact that because the cover was washable, you could change the look of your bedroom without a huge investment. Soon the convertible comforters (called continental quilts or sometimes doonas) were the bed covering of choice throughout Britain; their popularity soon spread across the English Channel through continental Europe. When the ever-stylish French adopted Conran's bedding, they called it by the French word for down: *duvet*. The name stuck.

Although Habitat arrived in the United States in the 1970s, it took some time before the duvet was adopted by Americans. While the duvet made a neat bed easier to achieve, getting the interior blanket into the cover proved to be as much of a challenge as making a bed with hospital corners. In fact, the duvet didn't make significant inroads into American bedrooms until the 1990s, when it was embraced and promoted by domestic doyenne Martha Stewart. A fan of the bedding, Stewart featured DIY duvet instructions in her widely read magazine and offered covers for comforters with matching pillows in her linen collection.

And while duvets are increasingly popular in the United States, they haven't quite become the cultural touchstone that they are in the United Kingdom. There, some employers offer their staff "duvet days," the equivalent of a U.S. mental health or personal day, to encourage better work-life balance: Without any prior notice required, employees are permitted to skip work and stay in bed—presumably under the duvet.

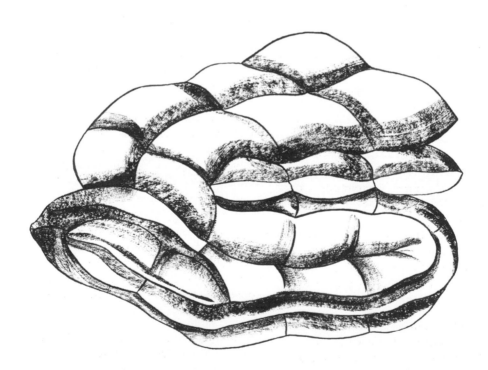

Fireplace

Since primordial man discovered fire, the pull of the flame has attracted all humanity. So potent is its appeal that the word "focus" is Latin for "fireplace."

While contemporary fireplaces are used mostly as a design and social focal point, for thousands of years the fireplace was a necessary source of heat and light. All medieval homes, whether a humble peasant hut or a great English manor, were built around a simple, open hearth—very much like building a campfire in the center of a home (talk about smoke inhalation issues!). Families would gather around the fireplace to cook and eat, tell stories, and sleep. It was so essential to everyday life that the hearth fire was rarely allowed to die out. In some homes, it remained lit for generations.

By the mid-fourteenth century, fireplaces had moved from the center of the room to the wall, and were added to bedrooms in addition to the main living space. This important development was enabled by improved, harder bricks, which made for more heat-resistant chimneys. In addition, a hood was added over the fireplace grate to catch smoke, much like the hood vent over the modern stove. Because they lacked an efficient flue, fireplaces of the time didn't provide as much warmth as the old open hearth. Bigger fires yielded (slightly) warmer rooms, and so wall fireplaces grew accordingly. Some were large enough to accommodate benches inside, so people could get as close to the flames as possible. These supersize hearths required a lot of fuel; many households went through one to two tons of wood per year.

For the next three hundred years, while fireplace technology remained essentially the same, decor became as important as function when it came to designing a room. Designers seized on the mantel as another opportunity to adorn a room and showcase materials—including elaborately carved mahogany, colored marble, and gilded decorations. The mirror-and-mantel combo still popular today dates back to 1690 and was made possible when the French developed the technology to produce full-length mirrors. Soon, the marble mantel with a huge mirror became a de rigueur feature for important rooms. The combination allowed those seated around the fire to look up and be apprised of the goings-on in the room at a glance. The fireplace mantel was also *the* place to display treasures. Small clocks (still called mantelpiece clocks) were designed just for that purpose. Porcelain vases, candlesticks, and candelabras were also given pride of place on the mantel.

The mantel may have looked great, but the lack of technological advancement in heating systems meant that people were still cold. The fireplace produced an uneven, shallow heat and drew cold outside air into the room. Smoke and ash were an annoyance, particularly in the eighteenth century, when lighter-colored fabrics became fashionable. In November 1750, King Louis XV's mistress, Madame de Pompadour, threw a party at her newly renovated château, Bellevue. The fireplaces operated so poorly that all the rooms continuously filled with smoke. The party was supposed to last for several days, but after the first soot-filled evening, her guests left to find clearer air.

By the nineteenth century, builders began to realize that bigger was not always better when it came to fireplaces: The larger the chimney opening, the more heat escaped up the flue. More efficient, enclosed wood-burning stoves began to supplant the fireplace in continental Europe, Scandinavia, and

VIRTUAL FIRE

••••••••••••

The Yule Log *show, a video of a wood-burning fireplace set to classic Christmas tunes, has been part of the U.S. holiday landscape for five decades. The now-cherished show was a solution to an understaffed radio studio at New York City's WPIX-TV Channel 11 in 1966. The three-hour loop consisted of seventeen seconds of fireplace footage shot at Gracie Mansion, the New York mayoral residence. It aired every Christmas until 1990, when it was canceled because the commercial-free program didn't generate revenue. But fans clamored for its return. In 2005, the* Yule Log *was back on TV, joined by versions on YouTube, Netflix, and Hulu. Now whether you have a mobile device or a plasma TV, you can spend Christmas in front of a fireplace.*

the United States (a bit less often in Britain). The stove was often the central feature of a combined living and kitchen area, and many incorporated hot plates for cooking.

Despite the availability of alternative methods of heat like central hot air and steam heat, the fireplace, with its unique warmth and light, remained a must-have well into the twentieth century. Architect Frank Lloyd Wright loved "to see the fire burning deep in the masonry of the house itself," and included a cavernous hearth (and sometimes four or five) in nearly every one of his designs. Throughout the course of his career, Wright designed more than one thousand of them.

As the twentieth century progressed, homeowners wanted the cozy ambience a fireplace gave a room, but didn't need the heat or want the mess that came with burning wood. In the late 1970s, fireplaces powered by natural gas or propane became available, soon followed by electric fireplaces with realistic "flames" in the early 1980s.

While the fireplace is no longer necessary to heat our homes or cook our food, it survives as a symbol of familial warmth and solidarity and remains a welcome luxury. Real estate experts estimate a fireplace can boost a home's resale value by as much as $12,000. Whether it's a clean-lined electric floating piece or a vintage stone surround with a gas insert, it can add pyro-magic to any room. It is, as Wright said, "The heart of the whole and of the building itself."

Flokati Rug

David Hockney's *Mr and Mrs Clark and Percy* is one of the most celebrated portraits in London's Tate Gallery. In the iconic painting, Britain's 1970s "it" couple—textile designer Celia Birtwell and fashion designer Ossie Clark, along with their cat—are pictured in their living room. Clark's bare feet are buried in a shaggy white rug. And not just any white rug, this is one of history's fluffiest: the flokati. Flokati fluffiness is fluffiness on steroids: The average pile is 3 inches [7.5 cm] high, while the best-quality version, tightly woven with the finest wool, can have a pile up to 5 inches [12 cm] high. (If you drop an earring in a flokati, you might as well forget about seeing it again.)

While that carpet may seem like it belonged to the era of sunken living rooms, harvest gold kitchens, and lava lamps, it actually comes with an ancient pedigree. Alexander the Great used flokati, the original shag carpet, to warm his campaign tents as he swept across Egypt and Asia Minor in the fourth century. The rug was created by shepherds living in the highest villages of the Pindus mountain range in Greece. Raising goats and sheep primarily for dairy products, the herders made use of the sheep's wool in clothing and floor coverings. After weaving the wool into a rug, the shepherds would wash them in the rivers that ran through the mountains. They soon discovered that when the rugs were rinsed beneath a waterfall, the rushing water caused the backing of the rug to tighten and the pile to become even loftier.

It took so much time and effort to make flokati that they were considered too precious to use on the floor; instead, they were used to cover beds and walls to keep out drafts. Prized in both humble huts and wealthy homes, these rugs were an integral part of a bride's dowry, or *prika*. In Trikala, a town in northern Greece at the center of flokati production, every traditional wedding featured a bridal flokati with a colorful border, designed to the young woman's taste and woven as a saddle blanket for the horse or donkey that carried her from her home to the church.

The flokati is one of the rare domestic objects that has been relatively unchanged from its original use *and* form. The international popularity of flokati has ebbed and flowed, but it reached a crescendo in the early 1970s, largely thanks to Jackie Kennedy Onassis. After her wedding to Greek shipping magnate Aristotle Onassis, she spent the first years of their marriage redecorating the Pink House on Skorpios, their private island in the Ionian Sea. In a nod to traditional Greek design, she layered beige and white flokati rugs throughout the house to soften the terra-cotta tiled floors. What was good enough for Jackie was good enough for everyone else, and the popularity of flokati exploded.

T hroughout the 1960s and into the early '80s, the handmade Greek flokati was joined on the market by wall-to-wall synthetic shag carpeting. Materials like polyester and acrylic had the benefit of being less expensive and available in any size imaginable. Perhaps the most extreme use of shag carpeting was in actress Jayne Mansfield's forty-room Beverly Hills mansion, where nearly every space was covered in it—including a Pepto-Bismol-pink bathroom—from floor to ceiling. That over-the-top use of the synthetic may have sounded the death knell for the real thing.

In the 1990s, designers of uber-hip spaces like The Standard hotel in Los Angeles rediscovered the flokati. The modern-day versions are still made in the mountains of Greece. (In the same way that Champagne in France owns the title of "champagne" for its sparkling wine, a rug must be made of sheep's wool and produced in Greece to be called a flokati.) The process has been modernized: The rugs are made on automated looms, rather than handwoven, and the wool usually comes from New Zealand, rather than Greek sheep. The final production step, however, is essentially the same. Called the waterfall process, it takes place outdoors. For traditionally white rugs, the water must be crystal clear, so if a heavy rain has washed mud and debris

CARE FOR A SHAG, BABY?

. . . .

While flokatis might be the fluffiest handmade shag rugs on the market, they are certainly not the only shag rugs. Sheep-herding tribes all over the world, like the Moroccan Beni Ourain, have developed their own versions. Unlike the mostly solid-color flokati, Beni Ourain rugs have black or brown geometric patterns woven against a white or cream background. The rugs rose to star status when the greats of mid-century design—Le Corbusier, Arne Jacobsen, Alvar Aalto, Marcel Breuer, Charles and Ray Eames, and Frank Lloyd Wright— worked them into their interiors.

into the rivers, the process cannot take place until the water is clean again. As the ice-cold water streams down the mountain, it is diverted into chutes that funnel into huge vats containing the rugs. The water pressure creates a whirlpool effect, which transforms the rugs into a thick fluff. The rugs are hung out to dry and then shipped out to warm bare feet all over the world.

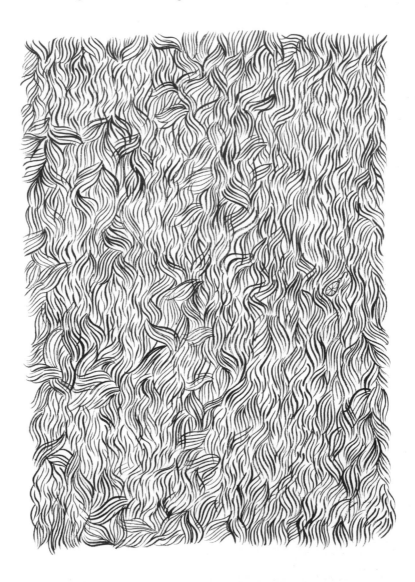

Floral
Centerpiece

If you're mulling over the perfect wedding centerpieces or simply filling a mason jar with garden flowers for a little tabletop cheer, it might surprise you to know there was a time when flowers were *not* welcome on the dinner table.

Floral arrangements for the dining table didn't become part of the standard tablescape in England until the nineteenth century. Before the 1850s, formal lunches and dinners were served *à la français* (in the French style). All the food was placed on the table at the same time, and you ate whatever was closest (unless someone passed a favorite dish your way). There simply wasn't enough real estate for fresh flowers. If there were any decorative elements on the table, they would have been elaborate sugar sculptures, porcelain figurines, or maybe artificial flowers. Real blooms were considered unsophisticated and, worst of all, cheap.

That all changed in the mid-nineteenth century when service *à la russe* (in the Russian style) became the rage. The meal was served in courses, which were brought out one at a time. Servants served each guest and left the dining room, taking the bowls or platters with them. To the Victorians, who preferred clutter to simplicity, all that newly freed space was a void that needed to be filled. Avid gardeners, they were inspired by the influx of new plants (like exotic ferns and orchids) brought from the European colonies, particularly South America and South Africa. The table was just the place to show off their latest purchase. To wow the guests at a dinner party, they placed silver wine coolers down the center of the table and filled them with pots of live shrubs or trees, often bearing ripe fruit. By the 1860s, artfully casual baskets of cut flowers, influenced by the French, had become the style.

In 1877, John Perkins, the head gardener at Thornton Hall in Suffolk, wrote *Floral Decorations for the Table*. The book described which types of flowers and arrangements to use for every situation, including breakfast, a cricket luncheon, and a family dinner. Perkins was best known for creating table-scapes meant to be appreciated from above by looking down at the table's surface. He laid down greenery, usually ivy, and interspersed small flowers like chrysanthemums on the tablecloth. The elaborately designed botanical patterns wove around small vases of flowers, candelabra, and dishes of fruit, only leaving room for the place settings around the edge of the display.

Other nineteenth-century floral manuals recommended a more conservative approach for everyday flora, like using low zinc bowls that could be painted

and filled with ivy and other greenery. In 1884, Mrs. Beeton advised in her celebrated *Book of Household Management* that ". . . there should always be flowers on the table, and as they form no item of expense, there is no reason why they should not be employed every day."

For more formal occasions, hostesses (and their florists) competed to create ever more elaborate displays, often encompassing mirrors, fountains, and candles. The truly ambitious, looking to ramp up the "wow" factor, even cut holes in their dining tables to insert a palm tree (or trees!), giving the illu-

sion that it was "growing" through the table. For large estates, floral centerpieces were an even higher priority. At Waddesdon Manor, the Victorian mansion built by Baron Ferdinand de Rothschild in 1874, more than forty greenhouses were needed to supply the orchids, camellias, and carnations that graced the tables of Europe's wealthiest family.

Floral displays were often so large they prevented guests on opposite sides of the table from conversing (or even getting a good look at one another). On the upside, they could also defuse tricky social situations when protocol, and not personal preference, dictated seating. At the wedding of Crown Prince Wilhelm of Germany in 1905, a Japanese prince had to be seated next to a Russian grand duke; unfortunately, the nations were at war. A huge bouquet was placed between the two men to serve as a buffer.

In the early twentieth century, the development of refrigeration technology made it possible to obtain a wide variety of flowers year-round. But fashion dictated that single variety groupings were de rigueur. Not only was it considered rather vulgar for different kinds of flowers to comingle, but it was also seen as a sign that someone couldn't afford enough of one variety to fill a vase. It was only with the 1934 publication of society florist Constance Spry's *Flower Decoration* that the idea of "mixed flowers" became acceptable again. Spry rejected stiff, wired presentations in favor of loose, fluid arrangements, using natural materials that were usually discarded, like grasses and berries. She even embraced using vegetables. Everything was styled in nontraditional containers, and she was known to raid her clients' cupboards to repurpose serving pieces.

While Spry's arrangements may not sound unconventional today, they were showstopping at the time. Literally. In the 1930s, Spry designed a scarlet rose and red kale leaf window display for a perfumery on London's posh Bond Street that attracted such large crowds that the police had to be called in to help with traffic flow.

Spry felt that everyone's life could be enriched by flowers; all you needed was imagination. These days, it's hardly a fancy party without some kind of floral arrangement in the center of the table; whether it's the formal luxe of a British estate or free and natural à la Constance Spry, any flower goes.

Fork

It might surprise you to learn that the utensil you eat with every day was once considered immoral, unhygienic, and a tool of the devil. In fact, the word "fork" is derived from the Latin *furca*, meaning "pitchfork."

> ## "The world was my oyster, but I used the wrong fork."
>
> —OSCAR WILDE

The first dining forks were used by the ruling class in the Middle East and the Byzantine Empire. The utensils moved west in 1004 C.E., when Maria Argyropoulina, niece of the Byzantine emperor, was married to the son of the Doge of Venice. Maria brought a little case of two-pronged golden forks to Italy, which she used at her wedding feast. The Venetians, used to eating with their hands, were shocked, and when Maria died two years later of the plague, Saint Peter Damian proclaimed it was God's punishment: "Nor did she deign to touch her food with her fingers, but would command her eunuchs to cut it up into small pieces, which she would impale on a certain golden instrument with two prongs and thus carry to her mouth . . . this woman's vanity was hateful to Almighty God; and so, unmistakably, did He take his revenge."

And with that, Saint Peter Damian closed the book on the fork in Europe for the next four hundred years.

For the next few centuries, the only utensils most Europeans used were spoons to eat their soupy stews or knives for stabbing meat dishes. Many people, even aristocrats, preferred to eat with their hands. This was actually a rather civilized practice, and hand washing was a ritualized part of the meal. In medieval France, for example, the nobility were called to dinner by a trumpet blast called *corner l'eau*, which sounded the horn for water, and pages would pour scented water over

HOW TO WIELD A FORK

• • • • • • • • • • • •

As forks took their place at the dinner table, the etiquette of use evolved. At first, the fork was held in the left hand and the knife in the right. After a piece of food was cut, the knife would be placed on the edge of the plate, then the diner switched the fork to the right hand to transfer the food to the mouth. This was the popular method of eating in France until well into the nineteenth century and is still practiced in America today. The English, on the other hand, avoided using the knife too frequently for fear of looking uncouth and violent, and so kept their fork held in the left hand, which eliminated the constant knife swinging.

upy treat stained fingers, slipped off spoons, and was unwieldy and messy to eat with a knife. The solution? The fork. As it turned out, there were more people with a sweet tooth than there were forks to go around. Custom dictated that a guest wipe the utensil off before passing it to the next person. Gradually the implement gained acceptance throughout Italy, and by the fifteenth century, using a fork had become a mark of good manners in Italy, rather than an instrument of the devil.

It would take another hundred years and another royal marriage for the rest of Europe to catch on. When Italian noblewoman Catherine de' Medici arrived in France to marry Henry II, the future French king, the culture, food, and fashion of Italy were legions ahead of those in France. Catherine brought with her Florentine cooks (toting recipes for ice cream), fashionable attire, the Italian banking system, ballet, *and* the fork. Adoption of the latter novelty, however, wasn't for everyone in Europe. Queen Elizabeth I of England owned forks, but preferred to eat with her fingers, as she considered "spearing an uncouth action." Finally in 1633, thirty years after Queen Elizabeth's death, Charles I proclaimed, "It is decent to use a fork," and gave each of his children a utensil set containing a silver knife, spoon, and fork.

the hands of each diner and provide napkins for drying before they dug into their meal.

It was the craze for candied fruits, beginning in the fifteenth century, that brought the fork to Italian tables. These sweets captured the appetites of diners in Renaissance Italy and changed dinner etiquette. Previously, refined sugar had been a limited resource reserved for medicinal uses, but expanded trade with Arabia and North Africa increased its availability. A favorite (and expensive) way to use all that sugar was to preserve whole fruit. The sticky, syr-

As forks began to be used more widely, their design evolved. The two-pronged fork was perfectly adequate for spearing food, but not well suited to scooping bites from below. In the seventeenth century, the addition of a third and then fourth tine made food less likely to slip through, and curving the tines slightly made it a more efficient utensil. Finally, by the end of the seventeenth century, the fork was accepted in the last European holdout, Scandinavia.

Americans didn't embrace the fork's use at mealtime until the Revolution. Prior to that the taxation (Navigation Acts) imposed by the British made it impossible to produce goods like forks in the colonies. The law required that raw materials from the colonies had to be shipped to Great Britain to be transformed into usable goods. Buying British-made forks was an expense and indulgence that residents of the colonies considered superfluous.

It took eight centuries from its first recorded sighting for the fork to become employed universally at tables in the West. And once it was accepted, no one embraced the utensil with quite as much exuberance as the Victorians. There was one designed for nearly every type of food: forks for eating lobster, forks for dipping strawberries in whipped cream, and forks for passing bread at the table. The range of varieties and rules were enough to make even a Victorian's head spin.

Thankfully, the pendulum has swung the other way in modern times. These days, even on the most formal occa-

sions, it's unlikely that you'll be faced with more than three kinds of forks: salad, entrée, and dessert. If you find yourself confused by the array of silverware at a more formal meal, you can always take heart in etiquette expert Emily Post's words: "Manners are a sensitive awareness of the feelings of others," she wrote. "If you have that awareness, you have good manners, no matter what fork you use."

Front Porch

The word "porch" is derived from an ancient Greek architectural feature, the portico. This was a covered open space in the front of a building, supported by columns. Both the Greeks and the Romans used porticos to create imposing entrances on important public buildings like the Pantheon in Rome and the Temple of Hephaestus in Athens. It's still used to impressive effect; modern examples include the White House, the United States Supreme Court building, London's Royal Exchange, and *L'église de la Madeleine*, the Madeleine Church, in Paris.

The portico was abandoned during the Middle Ages, when grandness gave way to a preference for security and easily defendable structures. It took until the sixteenth century for the form to be revived by architect Andrea Palladio. Palladio mistakenly assumed that the porticos he saw on ancient Roman temples had been used in residential architecture and incorporated the feature into his own designs, thinking he was giving his clients the look of an authentic Roman villa. He preferred the loggia, or recessed portico: a single-story room or walkway with pierced walls that was open to the elements. Both the loggia and the portico were more an imposing covered walkway than an informal spot for relaxation.

But these Old World structures were not the only source of porch inspiration in New World architecture. Today's porches were adopted (some might say stolen) from enslaved Africans. The first job for a slave was to build their own shelter. They built what they knew—shotgun-style longhouses with front porches. In their home countries, a raised, covered platform in front of the house was a way to escape the heat, and provided a respite from the nagging insects that flew and crawled along the ground. Porches were the center of family social life: where people greeted their neighbors, relaxed, and even conducted business. When European explorers and traders first encountered them, the concept was so foreign that they weren't even sure how to describe them to folks back home; one early European traveler called them "stages."

These raised porches caught on like only the best ideas can, and by the eighteenth century, front porches were an integral part of most American houses, large and small. It became the most democratic space in the home. While some rooms were off-limits for children (the parlor) and others to women (the men's study or billiards room), all ages and both genders were welcome on the porch. In the summer, it became another living room. Andrew Jackson Downing, a noted nineteenth-century landscape designer, saw the porch as an essential link between home and nature. It was a place for games, swinging, family conversation, and lemonade.

Unlike the later side porch (which was often enclosed by screens or glass) or the sleeping porch (usually entered through an upper-story bedroom), the front porch was part of the entrance to the house.

The decline of the front porch is directly linked to the rise of the automobile and increased availability of air-conditioning. People were more interested in protecting their cars, so carports and garages became the more desirable home addition. And if you had air-conditioning, who needed a porch anyway? When people did get outside, they preferred a backyard barbecue to a front porch chat.

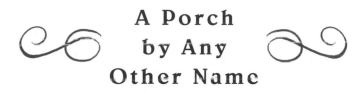

A Porch by Any Other Name

Gallery

Sort of like a wide balcony, this is the name given by French speakers in the lower Mississippi (like New Orleans) to the often multilevel porches that encircle their buildings.

Stoep

A Dutch term for an open entryway. It's the original form of "stoop," a landing at the top of the stairs to the entrance of a house.

Veranda

An open pillared gallery, often roofed, and partly enclosed by a railing. The word entered into American vocabulary from India (from the Hindi varanda*) by way of England in the nineteenth century.*

Glass Window

Humans need sunlight to thrive. Natural light sets our circadian rhythms, helps us make vitamin D, and enhances our mood. Homeowners and apartment dwellers covet it, and artists search for the perfect north light to illuminate their work. Travelers journey to tropical destinations to bask in it.

Once our ancestors began to build permanent, freestanding dwellings, they needed to find a way to allow light in—and let smoke from fires out. The first windows were little more than vents, or a slit in the wall. You can see contemporary examples of this kind of architecture in Puglia, a region in southern Italy. The countryside is dotted with white *trulli*, stone roundhouses, with tiny openings in the upper portion of the wall or a single opening in the ceiling.

It would take thousands of years for builders to figure out how to enlarge openings in walls without the structure collapsing. Early windows were open to the elements, or only slightly protected by curtains or shades made of fabric or leather. It wasn't until Roman ingenuity (and glass making know-how) that a better solution was devised (in the years ranging from first century B.C.E. to the third century C.E.). Artisans would blow a large bubble of glass, and while it was still hot and soft, spin it around until it spread and flattened. Multiple disks would be placed into a wooden frame mounted in a wall. The resulting window looked like it was made from the bottoms of glass bottles. Even if the view wasn't perfectly clear, it was a much better solution than a leather curtain.

After the fall of the Roman Empire, glassmakers used the same techniques to make windows for churches throughout Europe. Traveling artisans made colorful glass mosaics and stained-glass windows decorated with biblical scenes intended to educate the illiterate populace. Fabulously wealthy aristocrats and landowners had glass windows in their homes. Even by the mid-sixteenth century, glass windows were still so rare that when aristocrats moved from one estate to another, the panes would be carefully removed and stored during their absence. Those of lesser means, on the other hand, covered their windows with translucent sheets of parchment, paper-thin shavings of horn, or oiled paper. For those who had shutters, letting in light meant also letting in the cold, rain, or snow.

The biggest technological innovation in the manufacture of glass windows wasn't the result of the desire for more natural light in the home—but in the garden.

It's hard to imagine a time when an orange on the table in winter would have seemed magical, but citrus in the winter was unthinkable in most of Europe. Marie de' Medici, queen of France and grandmother to Louis XVI, craved the Mediterranean fruits of her Italian homeland, and she wasn't about to let the small matter of winter stop her. She had an *orangerie*, a specialized greenhouse, designed for the Luxembourg Palace that was modeled on Florence's Boboli Gardens. Lemon and orange trees were planted in large pots, which were wheeled outdoors

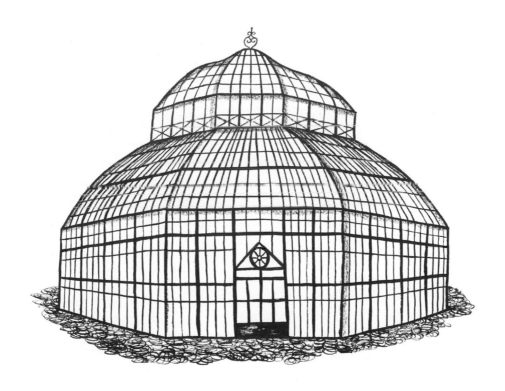

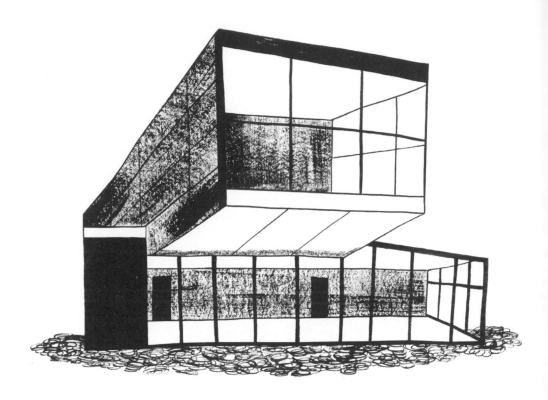

in the summer months and inside the orangerie in inclement weather. Her citrus desires came to fruition because the windows in the orangerie allowed sunlight to filter in and nurture the delicate plants.

Louis was just as obsessed with the fruits as his grandmother, and housed his trees in silver tubs. At his Palace of Versailles, his orangerie had more and larger windows than Marie's greenhouse. This was possible because of the new plate-glass technology that

was developed at his behest at the end of the seventeenth century. To create the large windows, molten glass was poured onto a flat, highly polished iron table edged with iron bars. The thickness of the bars determined the thickness of the glass. A heavy roller pressed and shaped the hot liquid into a large flat plate, which was then manually ground and polished. To showcase the achievement, Louis paired seventeen plate-glass windows with seventeen plate-glass mirrors in the gallery at

Versailles—which today is known as the Hall of Mirrors.

Now the race to satisfy the burgeoning market for glass windows was on. During the course of the next century, all of Europe vied to create the clearest, flattest glass on the market. And once again, the garden drove innovation. In 1823, twenty-year-old Joseph Paxton was hired as head gardener of Chatsworth House, one of the greatest estates in England. The small collection of glass houses didn't provide sufficient space for the plants that he was so avidly collecting, so he designed a massive greenhouse of plate glass and cast iron. At 277 feet [84 m] long by 123 feet [37 m] wide and 67 feet [20 m] high, it was the largest glass building in existence. When it was finished, Queen Victoria and Prince Albert drove down the central aisle of the greenhouse, lit by twelve thousand lamps, in an open carriage. The experience made such an impression that Prince Albert commissioned Paxton to design a structure with the most windows ever used in a building for the 1851 Great Exhibition in London. Dubbed the Crystal Palace, the magical structure was a marvel of engineering and British skill, built with three hundred thousand sheets of glass.

At the same time, the technology of steel production was leaping forward. Typically, wood-framed, load-bearing walls could be replaced by steel frames, and the walls themselves could be made of glass. This feature, known as a curtain wall, became a central element of modern architecture. It enabled innovators like Frank Lloyd Wright to create a relationship between interior and exterior spaces in a way that was never possible before, and gave new meaning to the phrase "room with a view."

Today, advances in glass production and window technology have given us windows that don't just let in the maximum amount of light, but are energy efficient, soundproof, and even hurricane-proof. They don't just provide a window on the world—but also protection from it.

Globe

Long before Magellan's expedition circumnavigated the Earth, definitively proving it was round, the ancient Greeks had spherical models of the Earth and the heavens. In fact, both Plato and Aristotle were convinced that the Earth was round. Just look to the sculpture galleries at the National Archaeological Museum of Naples, which houses a seven-foot-tall figure known as the Farnese Atlas. Dating to 150 C.E., it's a Roman copy of a Greek statue from the Hellenistic period, and depicts a muscled man who bends on one knee under the weight of the heavens. The celestial orb on his shoulders is the oldest spherical map in existence.

Knowledge of globes was lost for more than a thousand years, only to be rediscovered during the intellectual blossoming of the Renaissance. Early Renaissance globes were drawn, painted, or engraved by hand. With the mid-fifteenth-century invention of the printing press, the manufacturing process sped up dramatically. Even with this technological invention, creating a globe was a multistep, painstaking process that required first printing,

then carefully trimming, and finally hand-gluing maps over a sphere of plaster or a papier-mâché core.

The demand for globes skyrocketed as curiosity, coupled with new revelations from world explorers (this was the age of Columbus, after all), led to a constantly expanding geographical and astronomical body of knowledge. Even though they were mounted on an axis, early globes were made under the assumption that the Earth was the static center of the universe. The axis had nothing to do with the Earth's rotation; it allowed users to compute what time the sun would rise at a particular time of year and specific latitude. But globes were less a tool and more a way to express a growing understanding of the physical world. They were often a featured status symbol in Renaissance portraits.

Across the ocean, few eighteenth-century American households had globes, and those that did likely purchased them from London manufacturers. That didn't change until a farmer, woodworker, and blacksmith named James Wilson took a trip

A GLOBE WITHOUT THE MAP

· · · · · · · · · · · ·

The first snow globes were showcased as paperweights at the Paris Universal Exposition in 1878. But they didn't quite capture cultural imagination until 1900, when Erwin Perzy attempted to improve the brightness of the electric bulb. He placed a glass bulb filled with water in front of a candle, and as part of the experiment, poured a little semolina, the hard grain used in making pasta, into it. He was immediately captivated by how the floating grains resembled snow. In serendipitous synergy, Perzy was also crafting a pewter miniature of the Basilica of the Birth of the Virgin Mary as a favor to a souvenir-selling friend. He placed the church inside the semolina-filled bulb and wisely filed a patent for his invention. After World War II, the company, proudly named Original Vienna Snow Globes, supplemented the original church with Christmas trees and snowmen. Today they make three hundred fifty unique designs—and the exact components of the snow are a closely guarded family secret.

To scrape together the $130 (about $3,400 today) he needed to purchase an eighteen-volume set of the *Encyclopedia Britannica*, Wilson sold all the livestock on his hundred-acre farm. The next year, he made his first paper-covered globe, drawn by hand in pen and ink. Over the next decade, he took lessons on mapmaking from a local cartographer and learned to print his own maps, engrave his own copperplates, and even make his own ink. Finally, in 1810, he began marketing globes in nearby cities like Boston and New York. The smallest were sold at $50 each, which was markedly lower than the price of the English imports.

As education became the responsibility of the community rather than the family, demand for globes decreased. Though they remained a schoolroom fixture, in the home they were more of a decorative object than a tool for learning. Still, nothing quite captures the imagination like a handmade globe. Bellerby & Co Globemakers in London continues to make their products completely by hand, the same way they were made for thousands of years. The company is at work recreating a giant celestial globe that Louis XIV commissioned from Vincenzo Coronelli, the Franciscan friar turned cartographer, which is now displayed in the Bibliothèque nationale in Paris. The original copperplate for the 10-foot- [3-m-]diameter orb has survived for more than three hundred years, and Bellerby plans to create a

through New England in 1785. On that trip from his home in Bradford, Vermont, Wilson stopped at Dartmouth College and was captivated by a pair of terrestrial and celestial globes. He resolved to make his own.

new one that will hang from the grand staircase in the former palace.

If you don't have room for one the size of the original, Bellerby sells a desk version that will set you back about $1,300. Even at that price, they frequently sell out—proof that even in a world of virtual maps, a globe still captivates and reminds us how big the world really is. After all, whether bespoke from a London atelier, or a made-in-China plastic version, a globe makes it possible to hold the whole world in your hands.

Ice Bucket

Modern drinkers may prefer their red wine at room temperature and their white chilled—but that wasn't always the case. For thousands of years, *all* wine was consumed cold.

The Greeks perfected a method of cooling their beverages that required two containers: a footed pot with a bulbous body called a *psykter* was filled with wine and then placed into a larger vessel, called a *krater*, which sat on the floor and was filled with snow. The snow was collected during the winter and kept in underground pits packed with straw to keep it from melting during the summer. Drinking was done post-dinner in a designated room for the symposium (Greek for "drinking together").

The preference for cold wine carried from Greece to Rome to medieval Europe through the Renaissance, and at some point two vessels became one. An ice bucket could be made from almost any material, including brass-lined woods like walnut or mahogany, or marble (black marble was particularly desirable). These oversize coolers were made to serve a large group of

wine drinkers at one sitting; some were designed to hold upward of a dozen bottles. These giant basins did double duty: chilling the wine, and serving as a place for rinsing glasses between refills.

When they weren't put to work chilling wine or champagne, the coolers were displayed in the dining room or great hall as an advertisement of a household's wealth. And nothing made a statement quite like silver. In the seventeenth century, King Charles II of Britain gifted his mistress Louise de Kérouaille with a giant silver wine cooler that weighed more than 62 pounds [28 kg]. Even that paled beside the one

CHILL OUT

••••••••••••

To chill a bottle (or bottles) of wine, fill your ice bucket with equal parts water and ice. Add a generous handful of salt (rock salt is ideal, but any salt will do). The water melts the ice, allowing ice–cold water to surround the bottle. The salt lowers the freezing point of the water, which means the liquid can reach a lower temperature without turning into ice. When chilling champagne and sparkling wines, don't add salt. You need to lower the temperature more gradually to preserve the flavor of the wine.

banker Henry Jernegan commissioned on behalf of his client Littleton Poyntz Meynell in 1734. Meynell demanded the largest wine cooler ever made to celebrate the pleasures of the drink. It took four years to finish the 550-pound [249-kg] silver marvel. Decorated with elaborate Bacchanalian scenes and supported by crouching panthers, it was a miracle of the silversmith's art. When it came time to settle up, Meynell couldn't come up with the funds, but his quick-thinking banker made his investment back by selling lottery tickets for the container. The winner, Major William Battine of East Marden, Sussex, sold the cooler to the regent Grand Duchess Anna Leopoldovna of Russia in 1738. Since 1743, the cooler has been in the Hermitage Museum in St. Petersburg, where crowds still line up to gawk at it.

While the British were holding banquets, the French preferred smaller, more intimate, and less formal gatherings. Ice was a precious commodity, and there was certainly no point in wasting it if only one bottle needed to be chilled. Table coolers were typically produced in pairs with solid handles. Made from silver (or, less often, gold), they were frequently the most expensive component of a table service. Some even had scalloped rims, so that glasses could be hung from the base and chilled along with the bottle. By the beginning of the nineteenth century, it was considered chic to leave the ice buckets on display as part of the table setting for a grand dinner.

A lot can change in a century. By the end of the nineteenth century, the commercial manufacturing of ice for household use and the introduction of the mechanical cooling box (the predecessor to refrigerators and freezers) made ice buckets unnecessary. They were relegated to the back of the closet and fine dining restaurants. But if you've forgotten to cool that bottle of white or rosé, there's nothing like an elegant ice bucket for a quick chill.

Incense

While today we might think of incense as patchouli-scented sticks sold by urban street vendors and mall kiosks, burning this pungent substance was one of the earliest ways to scent a space. In many ancient cultures, it was believed that burning incense was a way to connect with the gods: The smoke would carry prayers to the heavens, and the scent, it was thought, just might sweeten the deal. Incense has played a similar role in nearly every major religion, including Hinduism, Buddhism, Islam, and ancient Judaism; the scent varies depending on the geographic location. In the Catholic and Greek Orthodox churches, frankincense-based incense (often blended with myrrh) is still an integral part of the worship service. (Both aromatics were highly sought after by the Egyptians and Romans.)

For the ancients, incense was more than a direct line to the gods; it could also signal the arrival of one. Cleopatra, whom the Egyptians believed to be a reincarnation of the goddess Isis, used fragrance to enhance the myth of her divinity, and to woo suitors. For the final 10 miles [16 km] of her 700-mile [1,127-km] journey from Egypt to Tarsus (modern Turkey) to meet Marc Antony, she lined both the deck of her barge and the banks of the Nile with incense burners. It was one of the greatest entrances in history; Marc Antony was surely captivated by her scent before he ever succumbed to her physical charms. Shakespeare imagined the moment of their first meeting on her Nile barge this way: "Purple the sails, and so perfumed that the winds were lovesick with them."

Incense also had more practical uses. In ancient Rome, home fragrance was an accepted part of good housekeeping. In the storeroom, where provisions were kept, burning incense sticks, powders, or cones served double duty: perfuming the goods and keeping away rodents. The Romans also believed foul odors bred disease, and used incense smoke to purify the air of illness—or even, for the superstitious, of misfortune. (The word "perfume" is a reference to that legacy, meaning "through smoke" in Latin.) Even poor families would keep incense burning in the entryway to protect the home against harmful air outside. Today, in the United Arab Emirates, where fragrance is an integral part of both personal care and a well-kept home, all the rooms (except the bathroom and kitchen) are scented weekly with the fragrance of frankincense, and on festive occasions, with oud.

> ## "It is a great shame, but of course there have to be some things in life that not everybody can have— and great perfume is one of them."
>
> —*DIANA VREELAND*

In the latter half of the eighth century, the Japanese began using incense to mark time by placing a stick of it horizontally in a wooden box with holes marked at specific intervals. You could tell how much time had passed by noting which hole the smoke was coming from. An incense stick could be made with a number of different scent blends, so that simply sniffing the air would indicate the time. (This scented method was so efficient that until 1924,

TOO MUCH ISN'T ENOUGH

· · · · · · · · · · · ·

Never one to do things by halves, legendary Vogue *editor and fashionista Diana Vreeland was as preoccupied with the scent of her home as she was by its appearance. She perfumed her impeccably decorated New York City apartment with burning incense, bowls of potpourri,* and *light bulb fragrance rings—all at the same time. As if that weren't enough, she would inject the sofa cushions with her favorite fragrances. Fragrance was such an iconic part of Vreeland's persona that her grandson recently created a line of perfume in her honor.*

geishas were still paid by the number of incense sticks lit during their time with a client.)

But incense sticks weren't all about business. By the end of the sixteenth century, as part of *kōdō* (the art of appreciating fragrance), the Japanese developed incense games: Participants passed around porcelain containers holding tiny slivers of scented materials and tried to correctly identify the scent. A favorite was onycha, the aromatic, smoky essence of a marine mollusk.

Today, you can still experience the ancient fragrances of Japan. Known for being inspired by "things that are a bit forgotten," Astier de Villatte, the French ceramics company, sells incense from a small island in Japan, where the sticks are handmade by the *koh-shis* (masters of aroma). As the story goes, a group of Japanese fishermen once stumbled upon a fragrant piece of driftwood. They brought the wood to the emperor, who was so enamored of the scent that he demanded it be reproduced on a smaller scale so that he could always have it with him. Sold in exclusive boutiques throughout the world, the incense, at $50 for 125 sticks, is a bit more costly than what you can find at head shops and from street vendors—but worth every sensuously scented penny.

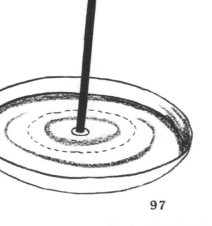

Jewelry Box

Is there anything more charming than a velvet-lined box filled with glittering baubles? From ones that play a tune to the iconic blue of Tiffany's leather version, a jewelry box is one of the few decorative objects that nearly all women have in common.

The jewelry box most likely came to be as soon as there were jewels to put inside. But let's pick up the story in the Middle Ages. Before safes and safe deposit boxes (or even locks for doors), home security was of utmost concern, and at the time, iron was the most theft-proof material for protecting valuables. Unfortunately, it wasn't the most practical option if you needed to move. Because portability was essential to the medieval lifestyle, most boxes for safekeeping were made of wood, covered with leather, and bound with iron for a little extra security.

During this period, a groom would often gift his betrothed a jewelry box filled with jewels (or perhaps empty with promises of gems to come). To emphasize the point of the box, the leather might be embossed with

appropriate inscriptions and scenes of courtship. A favorite choice was a quotation from the stories of Chrétien de Troyes, the twelfth-century poet: "Lady, you carry the key / and have the casket in which my happiness / is locked." A prospective bridegroom could buy boxes with empty crests that could, post-purchase, be hand-painted with his own.

The custom of presenting a lady with a jewelry box on her engagement continued into the Renaissance. In Florence, the trend was to use a rectangular musk-scented box, decorated with gold-leafed hunting scenes. A wounded stag symbolized carnal passion, so it was a gift with a little extra vroom-vroom.

Renaissance women didn't necessarily wait for a man to provide the jewelry (or the box!). Many women had boxes that hung on the wall in their bedroom next to a small mirror. A foot high, it would contain a smaller box for jewels as well as other items necessary to a lady's toilette: makeup, powders, sponges, and pins.

During the eighteenth century, bigger was better. As a wedding gift, Louis XVI presented Marie-Antoinette with a jewelry box the size of a small table. Made of tulipwood, it was balanced on delicately curving cabriole legs, embel-lished with floral porcelain plaques, and hand-painted with flowers. But even a table-size jewelry box wasn't enough to hold the jewels of the future queen of France. By tradition, the French royal family presented the new bride with all

the jewels of past queens—like a pair of diamond bracelets that cost as much as a Paris mansion. To accommodate the treasures, Marie-Antoinette ordered a massive "diamond cabinet." Eight and a half feet [2.6 m] high and 6 feet wide [1.8 m], with mother-of-pearl, sea green marble, and gilt detailing, the cabinet was as sparkly outside as the jewels within.

Marie-Antoinette had her cabinet, and Mexican women had their *secretas*. These low, square boxes on round bun feet were decorated with turtle shell, bone, and mirrors inlaid in geometric patterns. Although they were beautiful enough to be displayed, they were often stowed under beds or hidden in secret cubbyholes for protection from theft.

And it wasn't only the ladies who had elaborate storage for their baubles; young men were also dazzled by a little sparkle. After a stint in Europe to add a bit of continental polish to his education, the Scottish Duke of Atholl commissioned a small box in the shape of the Roman temple Septimus. Constructed to split open halfway to reveal tiny trays, the box housed the duke's collection of coins and medals. His favorite post-dinner activity was showing off the collection; the box was part of the show. With his elaborate jewelry box, the duke was taking a page from the lineage of the most dazzling of kings, the French Louis. Louis XV had a jewelry box that was large enough to be called a cabinet with blue velvet–

lined drawers to store a numismatic collection that celebrated the great events of his reign. His grandson, Louis XVI, had an astonishing medallion-decorated mahogany version that rivaled the one owned by his wife, Marie-Antoinette, for size and decoration. Each medallion was made of wax, feathers, and wings arranged to look like birds, butterflies, and plants.

In 1796, an invention by Swiss watchmaker Antoine Favre added another dimension to jewelry boxes. Favre had already developed a tuned-steel comb that made previously bulky music boxes portable and pocket size. It was incorporated into jewelry boxes in the nineteenth century. To further entice shoppers with money to spend, mechanical figurines—like a pirouetting ballerina or a singing bird—were added to move when the box's lid was opened.

The sales of jewelry boxes, both musical and silent, declined during World War I, when ostentation was frowned upon. Then in the 1920s, Coco Chanel made costume jewelry fashionable, and a golden age of affordable adornment began. A jewelry wardrobe was in reach of every woman, and remains so today. If diamonds (real or faux) are a girl's best friend, then doesn't she need a place to keep them?

Jib Door

Unless you live in a Gilded Age mansion, an old English manor, or the White House, you may not have chanced upon a jib door. Designed to be completely flush with the wall, without any molding or visible hinges, this masterwork of carpentry is often further concealed by the furnishings or wall decor.

It's more likely that your jib door encounters occurred with popcorn bucket in hand while staring up at the big screen, as they are often the stuff of movie plotlines. In the Batman film *The Dark Knight Rises*, three notes played on the piano in Bruce Wayne's library open the bookshelves to reveal a secret passage leading to the Batcave. While the mechanism that opened the door is a bit of movie magic, the door itself—and the passageway—are very real. The movie was filmed in England, at Osterley Park, an Elizabethan manor house redesigned by vaunted architect Robert Adam in 1761. Like many grand eighteenth-century homes, it contained hidden doors, a neoclassical architectural device to maintain the integrity of the home's design, ensuring that moldings or bookshelves weren't broken up by the multiple doors in each room.

And why did the rooms need so many doors? Privacy. Houses like Osterley Park and the Vanderbilts' Biltmore Estate in North Carolina accommodated a warren of back staircases and passageways that allowed servants access to the rooms without traveling the same path as those in the main household—and allowed them to leave discreetly if one of their betters entered the room. There were often jib doors concealed on the landings of large staircases for the same purpose. A maid and the master of the house running into one another on the stairs? The horror!

At Versailles, it was the royal family who wanted to escape the prying eyes of courtiers and palace visitors. In Marie-Antoinette's bedroom, two jib doors located on either side of the large state bed led to an exquisitely decorated series of private rooms. The queen, who hated being on public display, would spend most of her time in these more intimate spaces with her closest friends. The doors blend so well into the white brocade–covered walls that (unless they are left open) many of the eight million tourists who visit the palace annually shuffle right past them without registering their existence. The first room of the hidden apartment is a little blue library with a jib door disguised by a trompe l'oeil–painted bookshelf filled with faux red Moroccobound books. It was through this door that the queen escaped a revolutionary mob on the morning of October 6, 1789.

Like the residents of Versailles, other homeowners camouflaged their jib doors with faux books, and some used the opportunity to display their sense of humor. Charles Dickens personally designed the false bookcases at his country home in Kent and devised fake tongue-in-cheek titles (like the nine-book series, *Cats' Lives*) for the jib door that led from his drawing room to his study, where he wrote both *A Tale of Two Cities* and *Great Expectations*. Jib doors also abound at the great country estate Chatsworth House in Derbyshire, England (location of Mr. Darcy's mansion in the 2005 film version of *Pride and Prejudice*). In the home's library, a hidden door, disguised to look like a bookshelf, leads to a spiral staircase. The faux books filling those shelves were given humorous titles in the 1960s by the Duchess of Devonshire: *Consenting Adults* by Able N. Willing, *The Endless Road* by Wanda Farr, and *Venus Observed* by Sawyer.

JIB DOOR + ROMANCE

....

An exquisite jib door example is found at Gunnebo Palace, an eighteenth–century country manor house near Mölndal, Sweden, built for John Hall, a wealthy merchant. The Palace took twelve years to build and cost thirty-eight barrels of gold (when you're measuring the cost of a building in barrels of gold, you know it's pricey).

One of the home's jib doors leads from Hall's wife's bedroom to her dressing room; a landscape painting is hung over a concealed hinge, so that when the door is open, the painting is half-suspended in midair. The South American revolutionary aristocratic general Francisco de Miranda is thought to have gotten a good look at the hidden door to Mrs. Hall's bedroom on his 1787 visit to Sweden. De Miranda was so taken with Mrs. Hall that the colors of the Venezuelan flag (yellow, blue, and red) are said to be a tribute to her blond hair, blue eyes, and red lips.

The fashion for neoclassical design and for jib doors sailed from Europe to America in the late nineteenth century. Hidden doors were installed on both sides of the Oval Office fireplace in 1891, when the room was redecorated for President William Harrison by the Moses Company. There are a total of four doors into the Oval Office and five large windows; without the hidden doors, the entire room would look like a crowded assembly of doors and windows. White House architects seem to have subscribed to the philosophy that "you can never have too much of a good thing," as there are also jib doors in the private dining room, and two in the first-floor Blue Room: one opening into the Red Room, and the other opening into the Green Room.

In the 1960s, ever-chic English high society decorator David Hicks concealed an entire bar—complete with a sink and an ice-making machine—behind jib doors in a study. In another space, he hid a coat closet behind the same geometric wallpaper and moldings of the surrounding walls. In his own London home, a narrow entrance hall was covered in hand-marbleized bookplate paper that concealed a jib door leading into a small guest room. Hanging on the wall was an unframed portrait, but Hicks went one step further in his quest for complete subterfuge. Underneath the painting, he screwed a small vitrine table to the door so that when it swung open the table went with it.

While a jib door might add a lot of charm to a space, there is a downside. New York designer Albert Hadley (a Jackie Kennedy favorite) installed one in the red hallway that led to the powder room of his New York City apartment. The door was a little too well concealed and guests could never find their way to the bathroom. If you're considering a jib door for your home, you may want to make sure you leave your guests some clues about where to find it.

Lock and Key

The greatest luxury at home is not high-thread-count sheets or the quality of your crystal. It's the feeling of security and sanctuary that comes when you turn the lock of the front door behind you. While electronic access—key cards, keypads, scanners—have become increasingly common in hotels, offices, and cars, many of us still carry around small grooved metal pieces that we hope will keep us, and our possessions, safe.

> ## "I've got the key to my castle in the air, but whether I can unlock the door remains to be seen."
>
> —*JO IN* LITTLE WOMEN *BY LOUISA MAY ALCOTT*

Keys weren't always pocket size. The ones that opened the wooden locks of the massive marble and bronze doors of ancient Greek and Egyptian homes could be 3 feet [91 cm] in length—so heavy that they were commonly carried slung over the shoulder. Similar in size and shape to a sickle, they were decorated with gold and silver, and often embellished with ivory handles. Only the man of the house (who may also have been the only person strong enough to lift it) was entitled to the "power of the keys." The prophet Isaiah proclaimed, "And the key of the house of David will lay upon his shoulder," referring to this kind of door opener.

Roman inventors improved upon the design (and scale) of door locks by crafting them from metal. In many houses, locks were a simple lever mechanism; inside the house, money, documents, and jewelry would be secured in a lockbox. Romans often wore keys to those boxes on rings as a status symbol, because having anything worth locking up was a sign of wealth. Then, too, the Romans weren't big on pockets (a liability of wearing a toga). Men controlled the keys, and the power: The law allowed a husband to take his wife's life without due process if she committed adultery, passed off another man's child as her husband's, was habitually drunk—or had duplicate keys. (Protecting wealth was serious business.)

In medieval times, locksmiths tried to confuse would-be thieves by creating fake keyholes or obscuring the real ones with elaborate ornamental details that made finding them nearly impossible. Of course, there was a simpler option: require more keys to open a chest or door. In 1496, to protect the virtue of her ladies-in-waiting, Queen Isabella of France commissioned a lock for the door of their chamber that required five keys to open it from the outside. At that time, it was also common for the lids of chests with particularly valuable contents to be lined with *two dozen* locks evenly spaced around the lid. We don't know whether thieves were repelled by the thought of all that work or attracted by the imagined riches hidden within.

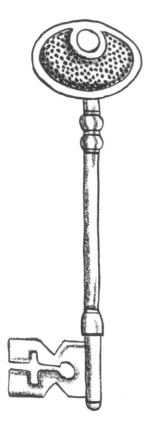

During the Middle Ages and Renaissance, keys still remained in the hands of the male head of the household. But upon marriage, the power passed jointly to his wife. Married women frequently wore ostentatious key rings on their clothing, particularly when conducting household business. It was a visual sign of a woman's social status and her right to spend money on behalf of the family. But it's unlikely that many women of that time were presented with a key quite on the level of Marie-Antoinette. "You love flowers, Madame; and so I have a bouquet to give you," said a grandiloquent young Louis XVI when he handed his nineteen-year-old bride the master key—set with 531 diamonds—to the Petit Trianon, the château that would be her escape from the rigors of court life at the Palace of Versailles.

During the eighteenth century, the concern wasn't thieves getting past the front door. Rather, it was the people already inside—servants, visitors, a jealous spouse. Locking furniture like writing desks and armoires became critical to keeping secrets and valuables secure. ". . . a man would grow pale if he forgot to lock his secretaire with the busy key that never leaves him. Love, ambition, and politics place their secrets under steel bands . . . ," wrote Louis-Sébastien Mercier in his 1782 *Tableau de Paris*. Locksmiths also got creative: "Detector locks" could keep count of how many times the device was unlocked, so the owner knew if someone had been prying in his or her absence. A French catalog even advertised a lock that could grab the wrist of, and fire a pistol at, anyone who used an incorrect combination.

Lockmaking was considered an art fit for a king. Louis XVI spent hours working with the royal locksmith François Gamain, who created many locks for the royal household (including a small iron chest for the king's most secret

papers, designed to be hidden underneath the floor). Though Gamain was employed by the royal family for twenty years, he eventually gave the French revolutionaries the location and key to the chest. The documents were used as evidence at the king's trial and led to his execution for high treason.

For hundreds of years, the simple lock and key remained relatively unchanged. With minor variations and refinements, it protected people and their possessions. But today, lock companies are placing their money on that changing. Electronic locks, with a whole host of authentication options including passwords, fingerprints, and smartphones, seem to be the way of the future. But no matter how advanced the technology becomes in an effort to do away with that little bit of metal, the purpose is the same: to make us feel safe in our home, be it a studio apartment or a castle.

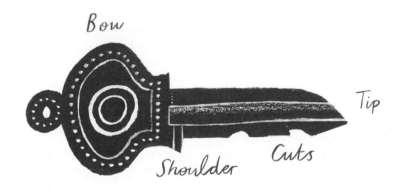

Bow

Tip

Shoulder

Cuts

Louis XVI Chair

Named for the ill-fated King Louis XVI, who lost his head during the French Revolution, the Louis XVI, or *Louis Seize*, chair is a timeless classic. Its clean lines and restrained elegance have attracted those with discriminating tastes for centuries, from Louis's fashion-loving queen, Marie-Antoinette, to modern-day designers like Christian Lacroix, who covered the seats of his dining chairs in candy-colored velvets. Today, if you're offered a seat in some of the most powerful houses in the world—the White House, Buckingham Palace, or the Kremlin—there's a good chance you'll be sitting in a Louis XVI chair.

The (relative) simplicity of the Louis XVI style was the perfect antidote to the curvy, over-the-top look of the previously popular Rococo style. The key feature of the chair was the legs—straight and (usually) fluted. They mirror the Roman columns uncovered in the ancient resort towns of Pompeii and Herculaneum. The first excavations of these towns in the mid-1700s revived an interest in ancient Roman artifacts and sparked an international craze for Greco/Roman design.

In other countries, naming a design style after a monarch would have been mere flattery. But in France, the royal family was the single largest patron of the furniture industry. The Petit Trianon, a small château on the grounds of the Palace of Versailles, was the queen's favorite escape from the boredom and formality of court life. There she played at decorating and redecorating the building—and keeping the furniture designers in Paris busy with a constant stream of purchases. In 1780, she ordered chairs and chaises "in the very latest taste" from designer Jacques Gondoin. With elaborately carved gilt arms and legs, and blue, white, and yellow taffeta upholstery, the chairs represented the high end of the Louis XVI style. And they had a price tag to match. The set cost 20,000 livres; by comparison, a "skilled" male worker, like a valet, tutor, or cook, would have been paid about 250 livres *a year*.

The extravagant high living of the French court, coupled with forward-thinking design, brought the Louis XVI style an international fan base that included Thomas Jefferson,

then the U.S. Minister to France. In 1789, after five years in France, Jefferson shipped forty-six Louis XVI–style chairs back to his home in Monticello.

After the fall of the French monarchy in 1792, the new revolutionary government was in so much debt that it seized all the royal property and art and sold it to fund the treasury. The market was flooded with art, furniture, and silver, and prices plummeted. Those chairs Marie-Antoinette ordered for the Petit Trianon sold for the discounted price of 2,530 livres. Many of the choicest pieces ended up in the hands of British and Russian nobility and can be found today in state houses and museums all over the world.

The lasting influence of Louis XVI style was propagated by high-profile fans like Francophile Jackie Kennedy. Jackie used Louis XVI–style chairs in the Yellow Oval Room, located in the second-floor family residence of the White House. There, even the coffee tables had the trademark fluted legs. She also managed to snag a pair of Jefferson's chairs for the White House, and later her New York apartment. They eventually made their way back to Monticello after businesswoman Patricia Kluge purchased them at the highly publicized Jackie Kennedy auction at Sotheby's in 1996. As for Marie-Antoinette's chairs? In 2015, a single chair from the set was sold at Christie's in London for $2,714,250: proof that great style can be a fantastic investment.

A GHOST OF A CHAIR

•••••••••••

In 2002, architect Philippe Starck designed the Louis Ghost chair for Italian furniture company Kartell, bringing the eighteenth-century neoclassical style into the twenty-first century by casting it in a clear polycarbonate. The chair instantly became a cult classic, with more than 1.5 million pieces sold since its release (there's even a miniature version for Barbie). Starck's elegant yet stackable chair is available in a vast palette of colors, from tinted-transparent tones to rich opaques. "When I started in design," he explains, *"a good chair cost around $1,000. I did not understand that. I felt deeply that it was not fair. Little by little, model by model, I took out those zeros."*

Mattress

Considering that we spend more than one-third of our lives in bed, it's not surprising that humans have always been preoccupied with what we lie down on at night. Today, our mattress options have exploded. You can buy your mattress at a specialty store, a furniture chain, or an online retailer with a dizzying array of filling options—innerspring core, memory foam, wool, or even horsehair. It's a far cry from the days when people had to save up chicken feathers from dinner until they had enough to make a featherbed.

The Romans, who lived extravagantly in most other aspects of their lives, were surprisingly spartan when it came to their bedrooms. The poor slept on straw mattresses set in a simple wooden frame. If your purse allowed, the frame was cast in bronze or even silver, topped with a mattress stuffed with wool or down. The bed—and only the bed—resided in a room called a *cubiculum* (from which we get the word "cubicle"), a small space with tiny windows that let in little light.

Later, in medieval homes, it wasn't uncommon for a semi-prosperous merchant family to have four beds in a single room. Medieval beds were big: 10 by 10 feet [3 by 3 m] was the standard size (much larger than the biggest standard mattress on the market today, the 7-by-6-foot [2.1-by-1.8 m] California king). They were so large that servants had to use long sticks to smooth out the sheets and bedspreads. Even if they had elaborately carved headboards and posters, these beds were essentially big shallow boxes filled with straw (this is where the expression "hitting the hay" comes from), covered by a large linen or hemp sheet, and topped with a featherbed. Because it took 50 pounds [23 kg] of feathers to make a single featherbed (that's a lot of poultry—one Canadian goose only yields about 6 ounces [170 g]), they were filled more often with horsehair or wool, which were slightly less expensive. If you had the money, you would layer featherbed upon featherbed, making the bed so high that a step stool was required to climb in.

Featherbeds made the English king Henry VIII nervous. Each night, ten attendants made up his bed with linen sheets, pillows, blankets and no fewer than eight layers of featherbeds. The king would crawl in only after everything had been stabbed through to ensure that an assassin wasn't lurking between the layers. In reality, it was more likely that vermin were making a home in the organic matter of the mattress and bedclothes; even the wealthy weren't immune to the indignities of sleeping with four- and six-legged visitors. Leonardo da Vinci complained of having to spend the night "on the spoils of dead creatures." Physicians frequently recommended stuffing garlic within a mattress or featherbed to repel insects.

> ## HOW MUCH IS A GOOD NIGHT'S SLEEP WORTH?
>
> ·············
>
> *Extravagant mattress spending in the hopes of buying a good night's sleep is not just a twenty-first-century phenomenon. The Swedish company Hästens has been crafting horsehair mattresses since 1852, and it is the bed of choice for a diverse clientele ranging from Tom Cruise to the Swedish royal family. Each horsehair bed takes approximately one hundred hours to make. And those luxury materials and time cost money: Hästens's mattresses range in price from $6,000 to nearly $100,000 (the higher price tag buys you hand-selected horsehair that is longer and straighter than those used in the less expensive versions).*

"The bed, my friend, is our whole life. It is there that we are born, it is there that we love, it is there that we die."

—LE LIT, *GUY DE MAUPASSANT, 1882*

Those big beds could get crowded. Our current custom of one or two adults to a bed is quite a recent phenomenon.

Even royalty had nighttime bedfellows—but more for platonic companionship than any kind of necessity. In Ireland, as late as the nineteenth century, whole families slept in a single bed. Etiquette and propriety demanded that the family lie down in a very specific order, with the eldest daughter positioned next to the wall, furthest from the door. Next came any sisters, by descending age, then mother, father, and sons from youngest to oldest. Finally, if there were guests, they would sleep on the outside edge, far

away from that (presumably tempting) eldest daughter.

Mattresses were not just for sleeping; they could also be an economic indicator. In 1848, when Napoleon III assumed power, the French economy was struggling. The government had a national pawnbrokers office (a mont-de-piété) where cash-poor citizens could trade their possessions for a small sum. People would drop off their blue-and-white-checked or striped cotton-covered, wool-stuffed mattresses—which are still made today—in the morning in order to get cash. With luck, at the day's end, they would have earned enough money to buy them back. But Napoleon understood the importance of a comfortable night's rest. As his first grand public gesture, he released the thousands of mattresses in hock to their owners. What better way to endear yourself to your nation than to hand out a good night's sleep?

In the 1920s, Zalmon Simmons introduced his version of the innerspring mattress. With coil springs nestled between top cushioning materials, they were handcrafted and expensive at $39.50 (equivalent to nearly $700 today). Simmons's "Beautyrest" mattresses were nearly twice as much as a stuffed version, so they were typically found in luxury hotels and the cabins of ocean liners like the Normandie

and Queen Mary. There wasn't much Simmons could do to change the price point, so he enlisted celebrities like Henry Ford, Thomas Edison, H.G. Wells, and Guglielmo Marconi (inventor of the wireless radio) to promote Beautyrest with slogans like "Henry Ford believes that even a machine needs rest."

A mattress is still a big-ticket item with a high profit margin: A bed with a retail price point of $1,000 only costs about $250 to make. But while your initial investment may be on the high side, take comfort: Most mattresses last about seven years, so your per-use costs are mere pennies for every hour of sleep (and less if you take the occasional nap). And a blissful night's sleep? Priceless.

Mirror

Of all the objects in our homes, the mirror is the one with roots most entwined with our ideas of self. There is even a developmental stage, aptly named the mirror stage: the moment at which infants recognize themselves as an individual.

> **"If we consider life without the mirror, we are only considering it half-way."**
>
> —*DAVID HOCKNEY*

Humans have long been fascinated with their own reflection. A classic Greek myth tells the story of Narcissus, a beautiful youth who was so enamored of his own reflection in a pool that he couldn't break his gaze even to eat and eventually starved to death.

Although still water creates a natural reflective surface, people wanted something less ephemeral and more stable to gaze into. The earliest mirrors were crafted over six thousand years ago from naturally shiny material—obsidian (a black volcanic glass)—or polished metals like bronze and copper. The invention of glass, which probably occurred in Mesopotamia around five to eight thousand years ago, was a huge leap forward. Even though the early glass foundation for the mirror was usually a dark blue, green, or brown, reflections were less distorted than they appeared on obsidian or metal. Glass also allowed mirrors to be made (slightly) larger. Still, quality control was an issue: Glass was sometimes too thin to stand the heat of the silver backing (applying a hot layer of lead to a hot layer of glass was a delicate procedure), and producing a flat sheet of glass was difficult.

Not much changed until 1450, when a different kind of glass trickled into the European market from Murano, an island in the Venetian lagoon in Italy.

After uncovering the secret to clear glass (a mix of just the right amount of silica, potash, and lime), Murano glassmakers turned their attention to mirrors. By coating the back of their glass with a combination of tin and mercury, they created a highly reflective surface. For the first time, people could see themselves as others saw them, without the expense of having their portrait painted. Cultural theorists like Steven Johnson have suggested that this new self-consciousness was part of the confluence of events that created the Renaissance.

Those who could afford mirrors became obsessed. "I had," said the Countess of Fiesque, at the end of the seventeenth century, "a nasty piece of land that brought in nothing but wheat; I sold it and in return I got this beautiful mirror. Did I not work wonders—some wheat for this beautiful mirror?" By the time the countess engaged in this transaction, hers was not the only fortune that felt the hit of the mirror craze. The flamboyant Louis XIV was spending the equivalent of $1 million a year on Venetian mirrors for his palaces. When Jean-Baptiste Colbert became finance minister, the budget line item for mirrors stood out. Rather than convince the king to buy less, Colbert wisely decided to bring the mirror makers to France. It would be industrial espionage at its most impressive.

To say that the Venetian government wasn't eager to let their cash cow go is an understatement. Workers were

> ### YOU CAN TAKE IT WITH YOU
>
> ·············
>
> *The elite Egyptians, Indians, Chinese, Mayans, Incas, and Aztecs all buried their dead with some reflective material. Even in death, those who could afford a mirror didn't want to be parted from it.*

forbidden to communicate with foreigners. Emigrating was considered treason. The offending worker's family would be imprisoned in his absence—and if that didn't bring him back, he could be tracked down and killed. Still, Colbert persevered in his efforts. Two years of secret negotiations, a massive amount of money, and a middle of the night escape later, a small group of Venetian glassmakers was installed in a Paris workshop. Finally, in 1672, the French mirror facility began producing Venetian-quality mirrors.

And just in time. Louis decided that he was going to transform his grandfather's hunting lodge in the town of Versailles into his dream home. The centerpiece of the residence was a glittering Hall of Mirrors, named for large mirrors positioned opposite equally large windows, creating the effect of an infinite kingdom. And those repeating images weren't the only illusion in the room. If you looked closely (and Colbert would have preferred you didn't), you might notice that each one of the seventeen large mirrors was, in fact, made up of twenty-one smaller mirrors.

The continuous 6-foot- [1.8-m-] tall mirrors that were the stuff of Colbert's dreams were not yet a reality. That technical breakthrough finally occurred at the end of the seventeenth century, when Bernard Perrot, an Italian immigrant to France, perfected the technique of pouring glass onto metal tables, rather than blowing it. By 1700, his factory was making mirrors that were 9 feet [2.7 m] tall by 3 feet [91 cm] wide. Paris became completely mirror-obsessed. Mirrors decorated chairs, desks, beds, candleholders, chimneys, and mantels. In a world illuminated by candles, mirrors had the effect of turning the lights on. Interior spaces reflecting sunlight were brighter during the day, and the nights glittered as candlelight and firelight bounced around rooms. Colbert's factory quadrupled their sales as French mirrors were exported all over Europe and as far away as China and Latin America.

Today, mirrors may be large enough to cover a wall or a door (or ceiling, if you're feeling naughty) or small enough to fit on the end of a lipstick tube. Decorators still use them to make a dark space lighter or a small room feel larger. As style maven Elsie de Wolfe advised in 1913, "Put in lots of mirrors and then more mirrors, and then more! Indeed I do not think one can have too many." Louis XIV would agree.

Monogram

The desire to identify the things we own is an impulse as old as humankind. One of the easiest ways to put your stamp on your property is with a monogram: two or more letters, usually initials, often woven together in a decorative way.

The first monograms were royal signatures used by Greek and Roman rulers that were stamped onto coins, using a pair of dies struck with a heavy hammer. They served as proof of authentication and identified where the money was made. Hundreds of years later, in the eighth century, the trail of Charlemagne's initialed coins marked his conquests throughout Europe.

By the Middle Ages, the monogram had become a practical stamp of ownership. In many towns, laundry day was a village-wide event with everyone's clothing and linens cleaned together in the village washhouse. When there wasn't much variety in the colors, fabrics, or styles, an embroidered letter or mark made mix-ups less likely.

Leave it to the French to take monogramming to entirely new heights. In 1547, the French king, Henri II, gifted his royal mistress, Diane de Poitiers, with the Château de Chenonceau in the Loire Valley. The epitome of chic, Diane wanted the château to reflect her well-cultivated personal style—and if she could broadcast the king's devotion, even better. She had a monogram of an interwoven *D* and *H* designed and applied to almost every surface: doorknobs, beds, bed linens, fireplaces, even the carpets, were adorned with the sign of their love. Unfortunately for Diane, Henri died in a jousting match and his queen, Catherine de' Medici, forced her out of the château. Wherever the entwined "H-D" appeared, Catherine had the *D* altered into a C.

It's one thing to carve initials on a bed, but terraforming—moving earth into new shapes—took things to another level entirely. Each sultan of the centuries-old Ottoman Empire had an elaborate calligraphic monogram called a *tughra*. In the nineteenth century, Sultan Abdülhamit II built a lake shaped like his tughra in Istanbul's Yildiz Park. On the tiny islands that made up the negative space, he kept a menagerie of exotic animals, including lions, giraffes, and zebras. Though the animals are gone, picnickers today can enjoy their sandwiches in the once-private walled paradise.

The Victorians, who took any opportunity to decorate a surface, were also big fans of the monogram. In *Appletons' Journal*, a popular nineteenth-century magazine, A. Steel Penn fretted, "From seals and rings, jewelry and watches, cards and note-paper . . . [monograms] have descended to . . . dog cloths and shirt collars, until there seems to be no spot left on which to apply them, unless it be to tattoo them on the forehead."

The Victorians were not alone in their obsession. At George W. Vanderbilt's Biltmore Estate in North Carolina, one monogram wasn't quite sufficient for the opulent two-hundred-fifty-room mansion. There was the familial mark, GWV, in an elaborate script that adorned everything from the tablecloths and napkins to the buttons on the servants' livery. The home's roofline was highlighted with a simple *V*, accented by acorns and oak leaves in gold-leafed copper. It is now oxidized to a soft verdigris green. George's wife, Edith, his daughter, and his parents all had their own monograms. Edith had the family's 1913 Stevens-Duryea C-Six touring car painted off-white with black pinstripes, and her initials applied to the rear doors.

Monograms can be practical as well as decorative. From its creation in 1896, the Louis Vuitton logo became synonymous with luxury. But the now-famous "LV" was originally developed to prevent counterfeiting of the Parisian company's designer luggage. Other designers, from Coco Chanel to Dooney & Bourke, have also used monograms to brand their luxury items. Today, a discreet monogram on the cuff or breast pocket of a man's shirt can (as it did centuries ago) prevent a mix-up at the laundry.

OOPS!

. . . .

When it's time to choose a monogram, think carefully. Traditionally, British married royals used two-initial monograms: the groom's first initial followed by the bride's. Unfortunately for Prince William and Catherine Middleton, in Britain WC also stands for water closet, a euphemism for the room that encloses the toilet. Not exactly the right tone to strike for a princely monogram. Designers spotted the potential for bathroom humor and simply switched the letters so that the C comes before the W. Close one!

Napkin

Whether you grab a paper napkin when you sit down to dinner in front of the TV or tuck a cloth version into a ring for a dinner party, you probably don't give much thought to the surprising origins of this essential domestic item.

While etiquette and style mavens may debate cloth versus paper, it might interest them to know that the first proto-napkins were neither. They were lumps of dough called *apomagdalie*. Used by the Spartans—residents of the military powerhouse city in ancient Greece—the dough was cut into small pieces that diners rolled and kneaded as they ate at the table, deftly cleaning oily fingers in the process, then thrown to the dogs at the meal's end. Eventually, raw dough became cooked dough, or bread. Because there weren't any utensils on the Greek table, bread served as napkin, spoon, and fork. Using bread was a convenient and tasty way to keep your fingers clean before reaching for a smear of hummus. (And yes, hummus is an ancient food, beloved by both Plato and Socrates.)

The Romans followed the Greek style of bread-assisted eating, but they were messier eaters—or at least more concerned about the furniture. Before taking their place on a cushion-covered dining bench, they would spread out a large swath of fabric called a *mappa*, a cross between a large napkin and a small tablecloth, to protect the seat from spilled food. While hosts often provided mappas, some frugal guests brought their own to fill with leftovers after the meal was done, making them the first known doggy bags. (Mappas were also used as a sort of starter's gun—dropped from the Roman Emperor's box to start a chariot race.)

Fast-forward to the Renaissance, when diners elevated everything, especially eating, to high art. Like the perfumed water they used for washing hands before the meal, the elaborate sugar sculptures that decorated the table, and the musical accompaniment that changed with each course (the first dinnertime playlist!), individual cloth napkins, or *serviettes*, became an important component of a refined dining experience. In fact, napkin folding became something of an art form, particularly in Italy. Starched and stiffened napkins were often folded into fanciful animal shapes, like two-headed birds, dogs with fish bodies, and crabs. But before grubby fingers could mar their beauty, the decorative pieces were cleared from the table and replaced with a plainer piece of cloth to sully.

Deep-pocketed nobility competed in such luxurious displays of wealth that even the elaborate art of linen origami wasn't grand enough. Take, for example, a twelve-course dinner given in 1513 in honor of Giuliano de' Medici (his father was Lorenzo the Magnificent, patron of Botticelli and Michelangelo). Each guest unfolded their napkins to reveal a little bird, which hopped onto the table just as the first course was served. (Whether the diners were delighted or unnerved by the surprise is lost to history.)

Napkins were also a highlight of the upper-class British dining experience. Affluent hosts and hostesses scooped up instruction manuals to learn the art of napkin "pinching." If you had the means, you hired a tutor for one-on-one instruction. The famous seventeenth-century diarist and Parliament member Samuel Pepys paid 40 shillings for napkin-folding lessons for his wife (a price that in today's dollars would buy you a pair of basic black Manolos). The napkins themselves were also expensive: A set of damask table linens, woven with a pattern visible

OLDER THAN YOU THINK

··············

Although paper napkins have been around almost since the Chinese invented paper in the second century B.C.E. (they were used during tea service), they didn't really take off until the 1950s. The convergence of dinner served around a TV and the birth of fast-food restaurants made disposable paper napkins the obvious choice for busy housewives. (Or anyone else who thinks life is too short to spend it laundering and ironing napkins.)

on both sides, cost about £10 in 1660, which could also buy you a good riding horse at the time.

The size and usage of these practical napkins evolved over time. During the sixteenth century, napkins were worn over the shoulder or arm while dining, then gradually moved to the lap over the years. During the seventeenth century, lap napkins ballooned in size; diners tucked the giant squares into their collars, like a bib, to protect fashionable bleached white linen cuffs and collars. Because baths were not a common practice at the time, those starched white collars and cuffs were the only sign that you practiced good hygiene, so it was essential that they stay perfectly pristine.

The Boats, Napkin folding instructions
from Mrs. Beeton's Book of Household Management, 1923

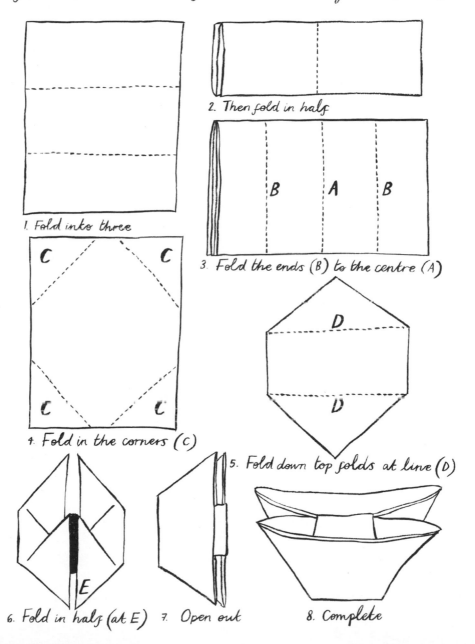

1. Fold into three

2. Then fold in half

3. Fold the ends (B) to the centre (A)

4. Fold in the corners (C)

5. Fold down top folds at line (D)

6. Fold in half (at E)

7. Open out

8. Complete

By the nineteenth century, however, those elaborately folded napkins were part of an over-the-top lifestyle that had begun to seem more than a little gauche. The traditional place setting style used today comes from the Victorians, who starched and folded their napkins (and sometimes tucked a bread roll into the fold). By 1920, Emily Post declared that "very fancy foldings are not in very good taste." (She also abhorred the bread roll in the napkin trick, believing the only result was bread on the floor.) Later, she would decree that napkins should be folded square and laid flat on top of the plate. For a formal dinner, Ms. Post's napkin presentation is still the correct choice; for a more casual evening at home, experts agree on placing the napkin to the left of the plate.

Whether you choose paper or cloth, napkin etiquette is still a topic for the Emily Post Institute and Miss Manners and hotly debated in the etiquette columns. What do you do with the napkin when you leave the table, for instance? Emily Post says to fold it to the side of your plate; Miss Manners, leave it on your chair. When should the napkin be placed in your lap? Both agree: as soon as you sit down. The question of how to manage your napkin (and in the process not offend your dining companions with evidence of your mouth wiping) is still hotly debated in the etiquette columns. However, as long as you're using your napkin as it's intended—to protect clothes and clean greasy fingers—history is on your side.

Parquet Floor

When you think about parquet floors, do you think of the peeling fake wood in your first apartment? Think again. Real parquet—a geometric mosaic of wood—is a wonder of meticulous craftsmanship, made fashionable in the seventeenth century by (who else?) French designers. The word "parquet" (pronounced par-KAY) is derived from the tradition of placing wooden planks underneath a throne, an area known as the *parc* (park) or *parquet* (little park). It elevated the seat of honor, both literally and symbolically.

Before the late seventeenth century, most Europeans lived in homes with packed dirt floors. If you were an aristocrat (or simply wealthy), you might use plank floors in the upper stories of your castle or home, and stone and marble for the more public spaces.

During the late Renaissance, when opulence and innovation thrived, wood craftsmen began to experiment with different designs for those plank floors. They also took advantage of exotic woods like mahogany and rosewood, made available by the expansion of international trade, and created designs using elaborate geometric shapes (parquetry) and scrolling arabesques (marquetry).

While these Renaissance artisans may have changed the look of wood floors, it was the French queens who put them on the must-have list. In the 1620s, Marie de' Medici, grandmother of Louis XIV, introduced parquet floors to France. She had them installed in the Luxembourg Palace by parquet technician Jean Macé, who was later appointed Woodworker to the King. Twenty years later, Macé laid a parquet floor in the Palais-Royal for Anne of Austria (who was Marie de' Medici's daughter-in-law and Louis XIV's mother). That floor was considered the wonder of Paris, and over the next few decades, parquet floors became de rigueur in upscale Parisian homes and elegant palaces.

Finally, there was Queen Henrietta Maria, daughter of Marie de' Medici and wife of King Charles I of England. In 1644 she fled to France to escape the First English Civil War. She spent the

next twenty years in exile at her mother's home. Henrietta must have spent a long time thinking about her mother's parquet flooring. Almost immediately upon her return to England, she had the first parquet in the country installed in her rooms in London's Somerset House.

Twenty years later, a king finally got into the act. Louis XIV (who shared his grandmother's, mother's, and aunt's love of parquet) commissioned sumptuous inlaid flooring to replace the leaking marble tiles at Versailles. The pattern, with its large diagonal squares, was inspired by the work of Renaissance architects Serlio and Palladio. It was so distinctive that it's still called *parquet de Versailles*.

Where royalty led, the wealthy followed: Parquet became a popular choice in upscale homes all across Europe and the United States. Both the complexity of the design and its laborious installation made it a visible manifestation of wealth and a status symbol. In 1804, enslaved joiners John Hemmings and Lewis (who had no known last name), working with Irishman James Dinsmore, installed a cherry and beechwood parquet floor in the parlor of Monticello for Francophile Thomas Jefferson. One stunning nineteenth-century example can be seen at the Winchester House in California. Beginning in 1884, Sarah Winchester, heiress to the Winchester gun fortune, spent thirty-eight years constructing her eponymously named mansion in San Jose. The house is known for its many dead ends, twists, and turns, all intended to confuse the ghosts of those killed by Winchester guns. Sarah employed a craftsman whose sole responsibility (for thirty-three years!) was to build and install patterned floors. They were made of mahogany, rosewood, teak, maple, oak, and white ash. Sarah's favorite motif was the one in her bedroom, which is laid out so that the sunlight streaming through the windows appears to change the dark wood to light and then back again.

I n the early twentieth century, woodcutting became mechanized, and mass-produced precut and prefabricated parquet "tiles" became available to homeowners and landlords. In the 1930s, many wooden floors were covered with then-fashionable wall-to-wall carpet or the newly invented linoleum or cork. This protected the fine work underneath, to the undying gratitude of preservationists and homeowners who prefer hardwood. If you're not lucky enough to find pristine parquet under your carpet, you have options, including the man-ufactured stuff. If you have the cash, wood craftsmen of the Renaissance ilk still exist. Based in California, Anatoli Efros, of Parquet by Dian, can install an exquisite handmade version using the seventeenth-century French technique. You'll be in good company; his clients include Steven Spielberg, Derek Jeter, and Giorgio Armani. Style that works for Derek Jeter *and* Louis XIV? Those French were on to something.

THE BALLROOM FLOOR

· · · · · · · · · · · ·

The distinction of most famous parquet floor has to be given to the one at Boston Garden, the home of the Boston Celtics basketball team. The arena was built in 1928; the basketball court was added in 1946. A postwar lumber shortage meant that long pieces of wood weren't available, so 247 red oak scraps were arranged in a pattern to get the most out of the material. The Celtics players, who knew exactly how the ball would bounce on different sections of the floor, felt it gave them a true home court advantage (about which opposing teams complained bitterly). No other major professional sports team had won more than five consecutive championships; between 1959 and 1966, the Celtics won eight. When the floor was retired in 1999, many pieces were sold, but others were incorporated into the floor at the team's new home at TD Garden.

Piano

You wouldn't expect to find a kettle-drum in the corner of a living room, or a double bass next to the bay window. So, why, of all the instruments in the world, does the piano have a place in our modern living rooms?

The story begins in 1688, when Italian Bartolomeo Cristofori was hired by Grand Prince Ferdinando de' Medici. It was a big break for the thirty-three-year-old harpsichord builder and musician. For three hundred years, the Medici family of Florence had supported nearly every great artist and thinker in Italy, from Michelangelo and Botticelli to Vasari and Cellini. Ferdinando's passion was music; an accomplished harpsichordist, he was renowned for his ability to play any piece of music on sight.

In theory, Cristofori had been hired to care for Ferdinando's collection of seventy-five instruments, which included cellos, violins, and dulcimers. There was a room full of harpsichords in Medici's Pitti Palace, but Cristofori was also encouraged (and given the resources and time) to create some-thing entirely new. He began with what he knew best: the harpsichord.

A harpsichord *looks* like a piano, but it doesn't sound much like a one. When one of the keys is depressed, it plucks a string and produces a sound similar to a guitar. The player couldn't alter the volume, and it was loud enough to hold its own with an orchestra. Christofori envisioned a new instru-ment that would be dynamically responsive to the player's touch, but loud enough to be played with the operas that Ferdinando de' Medici loved to conduct. He developed a system in which the strings were hit by individual hammers. The hammer would rebound, and the string would continue to vibrate. The harder the musician hit the key, the harder the hammer would hit the string, and the louder the sound.

In 1700, his new instrument, dubbed the *gravicembalo col piano e forte* (key-board instrument with soft and loud), debuted at Ferdinando's annual music extravaganza at Villa di Pratolino. At a time when possessing a new instru-ment was a bit like having the very

LESSON TIME

· · · · · · · · · · · ·

Emma Wedgwood, daughter of the ultra-wealthy British ceramic tycoon Josiah Wedgwood, took childhood lessons from the Polish composer Frédéric Chopin. Emma eventually went on to marry Charles Darwin, and she entertained her husband daily with her playing. Those recitals influenced Darwin's scientific discoveries; Emma was a crucial collaborator in his experiments on earthworms. She played loudly to see if the worms would react. They didn't, so her husband concluded that worms are completely deaf.

latest phone (pre-release!), the new *pianoforte*, as it became known, was proof of one's in-the-know status (and affluence). Pianos soon found their way into the royal courts of Portugal and Spain. Others were purchased by Frederick the Great for the Prussian court. When Johann Sebastian Bach visited Prussia in 1747, the king insisted he try out the instruments.

For the next hundred years, the piano was just a novelty instrument in court music collections. Then, a perfect storm of innovation improved the control a player had (allowing for quick key response and pedal dampeners for sustained sound) and that, coupled with a rising middle class (with more leisure time and money), pushed the piano's popularity to new heights. Composers,

who had previously concentrated on attracting royal favor and patronage, were eager to attract a mass following. Beginning with Beethoven, they began to create extravagant musical arrangements to introduce their compositions to new audiences. Musicians who could dazzle audiences with their virtuosity became superstars. Composer and pianist Franz Liszt swept through Europe, inciting fan frenzies at his concerts that would rival any stadium show today. Women would literally attack him: tearing off bits of his clothing, fighting over broken piano strings and locks of his shoulder-length hair. And, in tribute, many soon learned to play the instrument at home.

For girls of that time, the ability to play an instrument to entertain guests (and hopefully suitors) was a more important skill than reading. The piano was the preferred instrument because it could be used by an individual performer to accompany singers or as part of an ensemble. Smaller pianos were designed for home use: first square versions and later uprights.

Although improved manufacturing practices in the nineteenth century brought down the price of the piano, it could still take the average family an entire year to save up to buy one. It was the ultimate sign of success and refinement. In 1867, the *Atlantic Monthly* reported that "almost every couple that sets up housekeeping on a respectable scale considers a piano only less indispensable than the kitchen range." To meet demand, piano makers began to create designs that would fit anywhere. In England, there were pianos shaped like cabinets or bookcases. In Germany and Austria, they were curved to fit into the smallest spaces, and were made with long, tall backs. They were called giraffes after their resemblance to the animal's neck. There were even pianos that could turn into sewing tables with the flip of a lid.

For centuries, the piano was *the* home entertainment system. These days, with entire music libraries available at the push of a button, some people worry that we may be witnessing the swan song for the family piano. But perhaps because it's hard to do a sing-along around a speaker or dress one up with a collection of family photos, each fall children continue to sign up for piano lessons (and each January, adults put the skill on their resolution lists). And happily, there's a long list of celebrity piano-playing superstars who keep those would-be piano players inspired—and help ensure that the piano remains an essential part of the cultured living room.

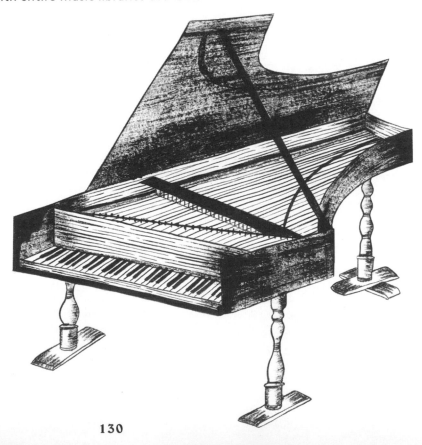

Picnic Basket

Light and sturdy, containers woven from reeds, straw, and other plant materials have been a favorite means of storing and transporting food for at least ten thousand years. And while we think of outdoor dining as a leisurely break from routine, in the past, it was often a necessity.

In the Middle Ages, peasants brought their midday meal with them to the fields. Lords and ladies, in search of a respite while hunting deer far from the castle, often stopped to eat in the forest. Before roadside restaurants and rest stops, eighteenth-century European travelers had to bring food with them; our modern picnic basket has its roots in the wicker hampers that they would pack for those long, horse-powered journeys. Aristocrats and royalty, on the other hand, traveled with elaborate dining sets like that of King Henry VIII. He brought one of rock crystal and gold on his 1520 journey to the court of the French king Francis I.

However, as all picnic enthusiasts know, it's the setting that makes the event special—and it would be hard to top the scene-setting ability of Alasdair Crotach, the eighth chief of Clan MacLeod. In 1538, at a banquet hosted by King James V of Scotland, Crotach was overhead saying that on the Isle of Skye he had "a greater hall, a finer table, and more precious candleholders." The king decided to see for himself, so the next summer, Crotach entertained the king at his manor on Skye. At dusk, the king and his party were led to the top of Healaval Mhor, one of two flat-topped mountains, and were met by hundreds of clansmen holding torches. Crotach grandly presented the spot: "Here, sire is my hall. Its walls are great mountains, its floor the mighty deep, and its roof the canopy of heaven." There was a meat-filled feast, brought to the site in baskets. Today, those two flat-topped mountains are called MacLeod's Tables.

When it came to the *pique-nique*, the French were no slouches, either (the earliest reference, in 1692, referred to a sort of potluck meal). In seventeenth-century

France, a favorite way for an aristocrat to wow the object of his desire was to stage an elaborate outdoor feast, or *cadeau* (the literal translation is "gift"). The food was transported in baskets by servants and artfully arranged on a blanket at a particularly scenic spot in the woods or by a lake, where the lovers would "accidentally" stumble upon the setup.

"The Rat brought the boat alongside the bank, made her fast, helped the still awkward Mole safely ashore, and swung out the luncheon-basket. The Mole begged as a favour to be allowed to unpack it all by himself. . . . [He] took out all the mysterious packets one by one and arranged their contents in due order, still gasping, 'Oh my! Oh my!' at each fresh revelation."

—THE WIND IN THE WILLOWS *BY KENNETH GRAHAME*

The Victorians took things a step further and embraced the picnic as a lifestyle. (There may hardly be a climate less friendly for outdoor eating than that of the British Isles, but that didn't stop them.) At a time when society was rigidly structured and governed by rules about everything from dining to wardrobe, the opportunity to eat outdoors (with proper silverware and linens, of course) while lounging on a blanket must have been exhilarating. By the end of the nineteenth century, picnics were all the rage for those in all the best circles, and sporting picnics—from cricket teas to boating suppers—were the height of fashion.

Victorian meals alfresco might have been informal, but they were not simple. In her 1861 *Book of Household Management*, Mrs. Beeton outlines the "Bill of fare for a Picnic for Forty Persons," which included cold roast beef, four meat pies, four roast chickens, two roast ducks, six medium lobsters, four dozen cheesecakes, and one large cold plum pudding. To quench the picnickers' thirst, three dozen quart bottles of beer were to be provided, as well as claret, sherry, brandy, and champagne. (You can only guess how many baskets were needed to transport that feast.)

As automobiles became a favored form of transportation, merchants like the department store Fortnum & Mason created to-go baskets packed with food and utensils. Servants would be sent to the store at 4 a.m. to pick up

the containers. (Lobster salad—half a lobster doused with a nearly equal amount of cognac—was a favorite.) Car companies seized on the car/picnic connection and made it part of their advertising campaigns. (Luxury brands like Rolls-Royce and Bentley still sell hampers designed to fit in their cars without rattling around.) For those embarking on a rail journey, chests in wicker or tin could be purchased at the train station. The container and cutlery would be returned back at the station on the way home.

Across the Atlantic, early-nineteenth-century American picnickers were mostly of the upper class, with significant leisure time. At first, they packed up their repast in simple household wicker baskets. But later in the century, high-end stores like Henry C. Squires in New York City began to market elaborate British "picnic sets" (baskets outfitted with linens, cutlery, glassware, and china) to the "most enterprising and wealthy gentlemen of the United States." As in England, car culture propelled the picnic forward into American mainstream society. Some of the first road signs were erected by automobile clubs to direct drivers to particularly scenic spots.

Today, the basket is often replaced by a cooler in the interests of food safety. While we're more likely to brown bag it on a park bench at lunchtime, or eat chicken salad out of a cardboard takeout container with a plastic fork, Mole's uninhibited pleasure shows

A BILLIONAIRE'S PICNIC

•••••••••••

In 1987, British luxury merchant Asprey made one of the most lavish picnicking sets in modern history for American billionaire John Kluge. The main basket was the size of a small U-Haul trailer and mounted on wheels; it could also be hooked to the back of a tractor or horse. It was made entirely of wicker and held fifteen wicker cases, each with brass handles and leather straps, and was outfitted with battery-powered hot and cold boxes for storing food, a water pump, and cases for enough Limoges china, Baccarat crystal, and silver cutlery to serve sixteen. A staghorn bar service and two folding mahogany tables with sixteen matching chairs, each monogrammed with the letter K, completed the set.

us that there is something infinitely civilized and utterly charming about unpacking a picnic basket and anticipating the feast within—no matter what the occasion.

Pillow

It is nearly impossible to pinpoint the exact date that pillows became an essential part of the nighttime routine. For those of us who spend half the night folding, turning, or fluffing our pillows in an effort to find the perfect sleep position, it's difficult to imagine that softness hasn't always been a bedtime priority. But for many living in ancient Africa, Asia, and Oceania, pillows were more like small stands or tables than the stuffed cushions we have come to rely on today.

Museums around the world are filled with carved wooden or stone "pillows" that have been found buried along with their owners. Some Egyptian neck rests date as far back as the Third Dynasty (around 2707–2369 B.C.E.). They look a bit like child-size stools with a curved piece resting on a pillar. These stands supported the neck, not the head—perhaps to safeguard the elaborate hairdos that were *en vogue*.

Traditional Japanese pillows, called *makura*, were essentially lightweight rectangular wooden boxes about the size of a large brick. A small oblong cushion stuffed with buckwheat hulls was placed on top of the box and finished with a sheet of soft paper, which served as a pillowcase. The paper and cushion were secured to the block with string. Some pillow bases were made of porcelain, which could be filled with hot water in the winter and cool water in the summer. They could also be used to burn incense or (for those who suffered from insomnia) opium. These pillows—without the opium burner—are still used today.

Across the globe, the Romans, fans of all creature comforts and conspicuous consumption, preferred soft cotton or down-stuffed pillows for both their heads and their bodies. The wealthy bourgeoisie and aristocrats of the Middle Ages followed suit, resting their heads on bolsters that stretched the width of the bed, supplemented with additional cushions. But not everyone approved of such a comfortable arrangement. Writing in the second half of the sixteenth century, priest and chronicler of Elizabethan English society William Harrison lamented the softness of (then) modern English pillows. Such indulgence was previously intended "only for women in childbed." Times had certainly changed, he wrote, when even men would not content themselves with "a good round log under their heads."

During the seventeenth century, when receiving guests while in bed was customary for royalty and the aristocracy, countess and renowned hostess Louise Bénédicte de Bourbon would receive visitors propped up on cushions in her grand crimson and gold Baroque-style bed (when pregnant, she even staged elaborate masked balls from her boudoir). Even her canine companions reclined on smaller versions of their mistress's crimson bedding in their elaborate doghouse.

Prior to the Industrial Revolution, pillows were constructed with whatever material was left over after stuffing a mattress—wool or (preferably) feathers—and were considered a true luxury item. (At the time, just having enough material for a mattress would have been an achievement.) It was only when textiles were mass-produced in the late 1800s that a cushioned sleep became affordable to everyone. In 1897, Sears, Roebuck and Co. offered their catalog customers sixty-three styles of pillows and filling options, with prices ranging from 45¢ to $6.10 (equivalent to between $12.27 and $166.39 today).

SWEETS FOR A SWEETHEART

· · · · · · · · · · · ·

If you've stayed in a hotel with turndown service, you've probably enjoyed the little piece of chocolate the housekeeper left on your pillow. And for that, you can thank Cary Grant. In the early 1950s, Grant was a guest at the Mayfair Hotel in St. Louis. He had his eye on a mystery lady (despite the fact that he was married to Betsy Drake, wife number three—of an eventual five). He set out to woo his latest love interest by creating a trail of chocolates from the hotel's penthouse sitting room to his pillow. The hotel staff, who had likely been tasked with the job of making the chocolate trail, were so impressed by the gesture that they began placing chocolate on all the guests' pillows. We don't know whether the lady was equally impressed—but the custom endures.

PILLOW

It was the beginning of the dizzying array of choices we have today that straddle the line between luxury and necessity—Sears now sells more than *five hundred* varieties of bed pillows. Today's well-dressed bed, with its many pillows, is an echo of the overly cushioned bed in the Baroque boudoir. We might not be receiving our guests propped up on pillows like a French aristocrat, but with a little help from the latest technology, we can receive the world: connect with family and friends, shop for the latest fashions, and binge-watch the most talked-about show, all while never getting out of our pajamas.

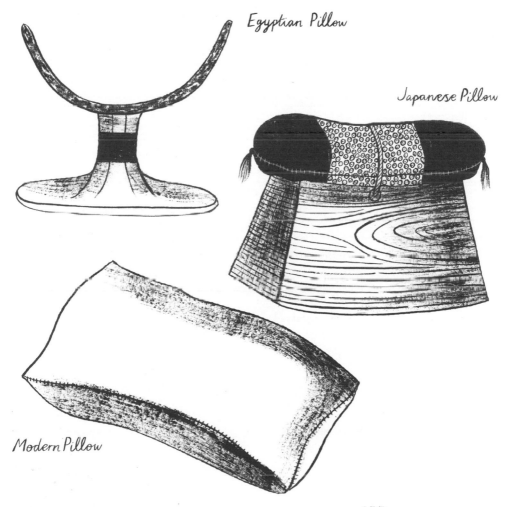

Egyptian Pillow

Japanese Pillow

Modern Pillow

Plate

If you enjoy slurping soup out of a bread bowl, then you'll appreciate the medieval trencher. These "plates" were cut from large round loaves of whole wheat bread that were aged for four days, then sliced into 2- to 3-inch [5- to 7.5-cm] rounds and piled with food. Diners would rarely eat the trencher; after the meal, they were given to the destitute, or the dogs.

The move from the bread *being* the plate to being *on* the plate was the result of the shift from eating with fingers to eating with forks at the end of the Middle Ages. Diners found that forks poked holes into the trenchers, allowing the juices of the food to saturate the bread too quickly. Placing the bread on top of a wooden base solved the problem. Eventually the trencher was discarded and just the underlying base remained. Carved from beechwood or sycamore, with an indentation in the center to contain sauce or meat juices, wooden trenchers were sold in sets of twelve and often painted with a floral motif. No matter how pretty the painting, eating off wood was considered déclassé, so more expensive

materials—silver, gold, or pewter—were used to create plates for the upper echelons of society. (The word "plate" originally referred to a flat sheet of metal. Only in the seventeenth century did it arrive at its modern meaning: a small flat dish.)

If your family fortunes improved, your first household upgrade would be your

USE IT, THEN LOSE IT

. . . .

After observing workmen using thin pieces of veneer to eat from during their break, Martin Keyes hit upon the idea of making pie plates from molded paper pulp. He patented his idea and in 1904 opened a small factory in Shawmut, Maine. Timing is everything, and after the San Francisco earthquake of 1906, the market for disposable dishes skyrocketed. Today, the company continues to produce a line of disposable plates, including the popular Chinet brand that graces picnic tables everywhere.

plates, both in number and in material. Those fashioned from precious metals were like a savings account that could be called on in hard times. Even kings melted down their plates to raise funds in a hurry, as both Louis XIV and Louis XV did when their state treasuries were depleted due to expensive wars.

Today, when we set the table for an elegant dinner party we generally reach for plates made of fine china, or porcelain. Europeans began lusting after the delicate ceramic after Marco Polo wrote about the translucent white tableware he had eaten from in the court of Kublai Khan in China. Among the spices, silks, and scents that he brought back to Venice, he tucked in a single example of the hard, thin, luminous waterproof material: a 5-inch- [12-cm-] tall, gray-green glazed porcelain jar. (That jar is still on display in the Basilica di San Marco in Venice.) Polo called the plates *porcellana*, a slang word for cowrie shells. It was the best metaphor he could find to describe them. Decorated porcelain soon became one of the country's most coveted exports, which is why many people today still refer to it as "china."

Although European manufactures couldn't quite reproduce the quality of Chinese porcelain, they certainly tried, and Renaissance Italians tried harder than most. They developed their own techniques for manufacturing earthenware—ceramics made of clay fired at a low temperature, and glazed to

TAKE ME TO THE RIVER

·············

In the 1500s, banker Agostino Chigi was the richest man in Renaissance Rome. To showcase his wealth, he commanded his servants to toss all the gold and silver plates used during each course of a lavish banquet into the Tiber River. However, though he was wealthy, he was also frugal. Once the guests had departed, his servants retrieved all the dishes with a net that had been lowered into the river before the party started. In addition to making an impressive statement, the stunt was also a creative form of theft protection; after all, no guest could walk out with a plate stashed under his arm if it was sitting at the bottom of the Tiber.

make them waterproof—that provided the perfect backdrop for elaborate surface decoration, such as a family coat of arms.

It would take Europeans a half century after Marco Polo's travels to crack the secret of porcelain production. (Spoiler: A type of clay called kaolin was the secret ingredient.) Once they did, manufacturers sprang up all over Europe to try to satisfy the pent-up demand for porcelain, which was so highly desired that people called it "white gold." Eighteenth-century French novelist Louis-Sébastien Mercier called porcelain a "wretched luxury," lamenting that "one tap of a cat's paw can do more damage than the loss of twenty acres of land."

By the 1850s, it was possible for the middle class to afford what previously had been the purview of the uber-rich. One of the rites of passage for a 1860s bride-to-be was to select a porcelain pattern for her new married life—a custom that has been retained even in today's cardboard container world. Our modern options for tableware have exploded, from plates made of plastic to paper and in nearly every geometric shape and color. Yet, odds are when dinner is truly a special occasion, you'll set the table with plates made of the same material that enchanted Marco Polo in the thirteenth century.

Playing Cards

Playing cards came from the only nation with the paper-making technology to pull it off: China. The first known cards, developed under the Tang dynasty in the ninth century c.e., were the size of dominoes. In China, card games became popular as an exercise that was thought to be good for the mind—meditative, yet challenging—as well as social. In 969 c.e., when Emperor Muzong capped off a twenty-five-day drinking binge by playing cards with his empress, it's doubtful he had any idea that his favorite pastime would travel the Silk Road through India and Persia before igniting a frenzy for the game in Europe.

As the passion for cards invaded Europe, the laws banning card play kept pace. Because cards were used for gambling, they were seen as antithetical to good Christian values. Bern, Switzerland, issued the first ban in 1367, based on fears of predatory cardsharps and a lazy workforce. The following year, Basel, Siena, Florence, and Vienna followed suit. In 1379, the Italian city of Viterbo passed a law prohibiting card games on Sunday.

In 1394, Paris enacted laws that forbade the lower classes from playing cards on weekdays. And in 1423, Franciscan priest Bernardino of Siena condemned cards as the invention of the devil and demanded that the repentant throw theirs into the roaring flames of the bonfire of the vanities, the *falò delle vanità*.

None of this stopped card makers, or players. In fact, many of the illicit decks were works of art. A design was cut into a block of wood and stamped on the card, then hand-colored. Some were themed, like one featuring images of falconry now on display at the Cloisters in New York City. The four suits are represented by hunting horns, dog collars, hound tethers, and game nooses.

In France, card makers devised the system of easy-to-reproduce symbols that we know today: hearts, clubs, spades, and diamonds. Rather than creating an elaborate woodcut for each card, they only needed to carve the picture of one king, one queen, one jack, and each number, and then stamp the suit on afterward. In the time a German,

Italian, or Spanish card maker could cut out every single card of a deck, the French card maker would have had a hundred packs ready to be sold.

The speed gave French card makers a competitive edge, and by the fifteenth century, France was the foremost producer of cards for all of Europe. Then in 1440, Johannes Gutenberg, inventor of the printing press, sped up the process even further. History may remember him for his Bible, but it was the playing cards that came off his press that excited the masses.

In France, the aristocrats of the *ancien régime*—not subject to the same ban as the lower classes—planned evenings around playing card games that lasted into the wee hours of the morning. The country's unbridled enthusiasm trickled down from the royals to all ranks of society. Any nobleman

worth the price of his well-coiffed wig would have feigned indifference to his growing (or shrinking) pile of coins or porcelain chips. But the money from a lucky hand could fund the lavish parties a nobleman was expected to host.

A favorite seventeenth-century game was the Spanish *hombre*, a fast-moving ancestor of bridge and whist. The name comes from the winner's cry, *Yo soy el hombre*: I am the man. Despite its difficult rules and convoluted scoring, the game took Europe by storm. You didn't have to be dealt a hand to participate in the fun. Being a spectator was nearly as good as playing (and a great deal cheaper). By the eighteenth century, the voyeuse chair was designed just for watching the action. The back of the chair faced the table so a card watcher could rest a knee on the seat and his arms on the top rail.

Some of the earliest known decks to roll off the presses were seventy-eight-card decks called *carte da trionfi*, cards of triumph, and were used in a game similar to bridge. Eventually the cards were called *tarocchi* to differentiate them from another game of trumps that used a fifty-two-card deck.

It was amidst this eighteenth-century French obsession that cards began to be used for divination. First, Jean-Baptiste Alliette published *Etteilla, or a Way to Entertain Yourself with a Deck of Cards*. His first book instructed would-be fortune-tellers on how to use a standard card deck

for prophecy. Then in 1781, Count de Gébelin and Comte de Mellet (who, as far as history tells us, did nothing else of note) wrote an essay in which they postulated that the tarocchi held the secrets of ancient Egypt and could foretell the future.

Our modern deck—fifty-two cards split evenly among four suits—descends directly from the ones used by the high-rolling French (when they were playing cards and not telling fortunes). If you have cards stashed somewhere, there's a good chance it's a red or blue Bicycle set. Named for the cyclist on the back of the cards, they were first manufactured in 1885 in Cincinnati, when cycling was a newfangled pastime. These iconic cards are a favorite of Las Vegas casinos—a strong endorsement considering the average casino goes through three hundred thousand packs per year.

Whether your game is canasta, bridge, poker, or Go Fish, remember that Lady Luck never goes out of style.

Potpourri

One of the simpler ways to ensure your surroundings smell sweet is to bring fresh, good-smelling things from the garden indoors. In ancient Egypt, Hebrew wives threw mint on their hard dirt floors. The Romans spread aromatic leaves like verbena and myrtle on the floor so that guests would crush them as they walked and release their scent. In India, whole, dried, violet-scented orris root was placed in the sun blinds and watered throughout the day; the rehydrated roots released their perfume while the process of evaporation helped cool the home.

In medieval Europe, homemakers favored chamomile, which released a heady apple scent when crushed. They also stashed fragrant leaves behind cushions, where the scent was released when anyone sat down. At some point, someone figured out that dried plants were just as fragrant as fresh, and stuffed sachets with flowers and herbs, which were then tucked into clothes chests to deter moths and keep garments smelling sweet.

For those with deep pockets, professional perfumers traveled from castle to castle. They created custom blends of dried leaves and petals, often adding exotic spices to the mix. Crushing the mixture into a powder concentrated the scent and made it more intense. Some blends were even thought to have therapeutic properties: During the fourteenth century, when the Black Death swept through Europe, camphor and cloves were used to fumigate rooms or ward off the disease.

What went into potpourri depended on personal taste and fashion of the time. In the Renaissance, musky animal scents utilizing musk deer and civet were all the rage (capturing these smells involved extracting the scents from the animal's glands). Henry VIII and his daughter Elizabeth I of England were fond of a blend of rose and musk. King Henry IV of France used a mixture of powdered orris root and sandalwood to perfume his household linen. And seventeenth-century French foreign policy mastermind Cardinal Richelieu (remember *The Three Musketeers*?) used bellows to fumigate his room daily with floral powders.

Potpourri was especially useful in a time when hygiene was less than stellar. Imagine the overwhelming smell of unbathed bodies and streets used as sewers. During the reign of Charles I in mid-seventeenth-century England, potpourri rings—a small, lidded box of fragrant powder attached to a ring—were popular for both sexes. The wearer could inconspicuously bring their hand to their nose, open the box with a flick of the thumb, and inhale the scent. Some rings were perforated so the scent could escape without even needing to lift the lid. No matter how rank the odor of the room or your companions, at least *you* were surrounded by a pleasant smell.

Potpourri's move from powders and sachets to bowls was the result of a convergence of two English trends: the eighteenth-century craze for porcelain and the fashion for botanical scents, particularly jasmine. Simultaneously, the European desire for Eastern luxury goods had exploded—especially spices, tea, and silk. These three commodities had to be transported above the ship's waterline, leaving plenty of cargo space below for porcelain vases. These were the perfect vessels for jasmine-scented potpourri, a mixture of dried flowers doused with jasmine essential oil (which helped the dried flowers retain their scent longer). Potpourri jars—tall, urnlike vases (some 3 feet [91 cm]

ANCIENT AROMAS WITH MODERN APPEAL

Vogue editors, lifestyle gurus like Olivia Palermo and Inès de la Fressange, movie stars like Catherine Zeta-Jones, and royalty like Princess Caroline of Monaco are obsessed with the pot-pourri from Farmaceutica di Santa Maria Novella. One of the world's oldest pharmacies, this Florentine institution still makes their traditional potpourri in large terra-cotta vats, just as they have been doing since they opened their doors in 1612. Their signature potpourri— a strong but subtle fragrance with notes of sandalwood and orange—is made from a secret recipe of flowers and herbs sourced from the pharmacy's own garden and is packed in hand-embroidered silk sachets.

high!) with pierced lids that allowed the scent to escape—quickly became all the rage.

The Victorians wholeheartedly embraced potpourri. Housewives and ladies made their own with dried flowers and essential oils, or purchased ready-made versions from shops like Taylors of London, which created customized mixes that were guaranteed to retain their scent for fifty years. When the fussy, cluttered Victorian style fell out of fashion in favor of the cleaner lines of the Edwardian era, potpourri was considered as outdated as tassels on a velvet sofa.

While potpourri never went away entirely, it took a back seat to more modern (and convenient) forms of room fragrance like sprays. It was so unfamiliar to most people that at a New York City cocktail party in 1974, designer Barbara Milo Ohrbach watched in horror as a couple of guests munched potpourri as if it were a fancy trail mix. But by the 1980s, it had become a mass-market commodity. Cheaper mixtures were augmented with artificially scented wood chips that were dyed colors not found in nature.

Today we're more likely to burn a scented candle or use an electric diffuser to imbue our personal space. But if you're in the mood for a simple and satisfying DIY project, try creating your own unique blend of colors and aromas to display in a pretty jar or bowl. There's no more personal way to make your home your own.

Punch Bowl

Unless you got one as a wedding present, or inherited your Aunt Ida's, the last time you saw a punch bowl was probably at your senior prom. But that just might be changing: Punch and its accoutrements are making a comeback. And if you've ever been stuck behind the bar mixing individual drinks for a thirsty crowd, you'll understand the revived allure.

Punch burst onto the European scene in the late seventeenth century, when the pace of trade between India and Britain exploded. Silk, raw cotton, indigo, tea, spices, and opium were on the long list of goods that poured into Britain from India. That list, the theory goes, also included punch. The word is thought be derived from the Hindi word for "five," *pac*, which refers to the five ingredients in the original Indian recipe: arrack (a spirit so unpleasant it wasn't palatable straight), sugar, lemon or lime, nutmeg and other spices, and water. Usually made in quantity, it was intended to be drunk communally. It's difficult to pin down the drink's inventor; credit seems to have gotten lost in the haze of inebriation. But from the

1670s to the 1850s, punch topped the drink list of Europe.

Unlike our ice-cold (and sometimes sherbet-filled) bowls, the first versions of punch were always served hot. The earliest punch bowls weren't exercises in silversmithing or cut-glass crystal, but rather creamware, a type of glazed earthenware made by combining white-firing clays and calcined flint. The material was both easy to clean and heat resistant.

As the popularity of punch expanded westward from India into Europe and North America, punch bowls became a standard serving piece in homes and local drinking establishments. In fact, most taverns possessed practically equal numbers of punch bowls and benches.

American punches of the Colonial era used cheap and widely available rum as a base. It could be mixed with water and fruit juice to make a cold summer drink, or with sugar and spices for a warming winter one. Drinking was considered the purview of menfolk. After dinner, the women retired to the drawing room and the bowl would be placed in the center of the dining table for the men to consume.

Across the pond in Britain, punch bowls reached mammoth proportions. In the early 1760s, Francis Greville (later the Earl of Warwick) held a party to celebrate the birth of his son. The guest list topped six thousand, and the punch bowl would probably make the *Guinness Book of World Records* today. The giant marble basin was filled with a mixture made from 25,000 lemons, 80 pints [38 L] of lemon juice, 4 large barrels of water, 50 tons [45 t] of sugar, 300 biscuits, 5 pounds [2.3 kg] of nutmeg, and about 145 gallons [549 L] of Malaga wine. Everyone was very happy.

By the beginning of the eighteenth century, if you could afford it, silver was the punch bowl material of choice. Perhaps the most famous is the one that Paul Revere made for the Sons of Liberty in 1768. It's engraved with the names of the secret patriotic society's fifteen members and a message in celebration of the Massachusetts House of Representatives' vote against repressive British policies.

Then in the mid-nineteenth century, almost as suddenly as it became a party essential, the punch bowl made an exit. The demise of punch-fueled revelries was probably due to better distilling methods, which meant spirits required less doctoring to make them palatable. There was also an increase in the variety of alcoholic beverages on the market.

THE MOST FAMOUS PUNCH BOWL IN SPORTS

• • • • • • • • • • • •

In 1886, the British politician Lord Frederick Stanley arrived in Canada to represent Queen Victoria's interest in the colony. He fell head over heels for its natural beauty, the fishing, and the (then) new sport of ice hockey. His sons took up the sport, and Stanley and his wife became avid fans. Proud parent that he was, he felt a little cheated that the sport didn't have a final championship, or even a trophy.

Lord Stanley decided to do something about that, and the Stanley Cup was born. He bought a silver punch bowl in London for the equivalent of $1,000 today and had "Dominion Hockey Challenge Cup" inscribed on one side and "From Stanley of Preston" on the other. The only stipulation was that the cup would be passed each year to the championship team.

Lord Stanley never got to see the cup awarded. The month after he bought it, his brother died. He returned to England and never visited Canada again.

Today, punch is popular once more. Besides being easier on the host, a punch bowl brings a festive flair to a gathering that you don't get with scotch on the rocks. Maybe Aunt Ida was on to something.

American Orange Punch

This recipe was served by the barrel at the 1829 White House inaugural reception for Andrew Jackson, seventh president of the United States.

4 oranges

3/4 cup [150 g] light raw sugar, plus more as needed

56 fluid ounces [1.7 L] boiling water

12 to 16 fluid ounces [360 to 480 ml] brandy

12 to 16 fluid ounces [360 to 480 ml] Jamaican rum

8 fluid ounces [240 ml] porter beer

1 ounce [30 ml] Curaçao, noyaux, or maraschino liqueur (optional)

1. Using a vegetable peeler or paring knife, remove the peel from two of the oranges.

2. Combine the peels and sugar in a large, heatproof, nonreactive bowl. Allow to sit for 1 hour.

3. Juice all of the oranges. Add the juice and boiling water to the sugar and peels. Allow to infuse for 30 minutes.

4. Strain the orange mixture into a punch bowl and add the brandy, rum, porter, and other liquors, if using. Sample and adjust with water or sugar to taste.

5. Add ice, and enjoy.

Rocking Chair

A mash-up of the cradle and chair, the rocker is a relatively recent invention, created in the eighteenth century.

Cradles on curved supports have lulled infants to sleep since the Middle Ages. Why it took so long for adults to get in on the game—and who actually crafted the first rocking chair—remains a bit of a mystery. Noted architectural historian Witold Rybczynski suggests that the lack of a light and inexpensive chair might have kept would-be rockers from seated bliss. Reserved for kings, queens, lords, and ladies, medieval chairs were too heavy and unwieldy to be supported by rocking legs. And it is nearly impossible to imagine a gilded Louis XIV chair with rockers—how undignified.

But for a colonial settler in the North American wilderness, dignity and hierarchy were less of a concern. By the mid-eighteenth century, the great Philadelphia furniture makers were selling "rocking nurse chairs." Originally intended for use by nursing mothers, the elderly, and the ill, they were soon a part of almost every American home.

First relegated to nurseries and sickrooms, they soon found their way into parlors, bedrooms, and kitchens and, of course, onto porches. There were versions made from rattan and wicker, rush-bottomed chairs, and others that were fully upholstered.

Foreign visitors found rocking chairs exotic enough to write home about. Philip Schaff, a Swiss theologian who spent most of his life in the United States, considered the rocking chair to be a reflection of the national character. "Even when seated, [Americans] push themselves to and fro in their rocking chairs," he wrote in 1854. "They live in a state of perpetual excitement in their business, their politics and their religion."

The rocker was as at home on Main Street as it was in the White House: Abraham Lincoln, William McKinley, and Teddy Roosevelt all spent time rocking. (In fact, President Lincoln was seated in an upholstered rocking chair in Ford's Theater when he was assassinated.) Calvin Coolidge smoked cigars and watched the setting sun and

ROCKER ROYALTY

· · · · · · · · · · · ·

Though the rocking chair was born in America, it was a German–Austrian furniture maker who gave it some European sophistication and polish. After seeing metal rockers at the show–stopping London exhibition of modern industrial technology and design in 1851, Michael Thonet created a sinuous wood version. To do so, he invented a process that used steam to bend solid wood, enabling curved chair backs and legs. Thirty years before Henry Ford, he created an assembly line to produce his chairs. Rockers had not been popular in Europe, but Thonet's bentwood version changed that. The chair became a favorite of the Impressionists and appeared in the paintings of Renoir, Vuillard, and Tissot. Picasso and Miró both kept Thonet rockers in their studios. But you don't have to be an artist to appreciate the elegant lines of a Thonet rocking chair. It remains a simple way to add a stylish touch to any room today.

passing streetcars from his straight-backed rocker on the White House North Portico. Harry Truman had several on the first-floor balcony he built off the Yellow Oval Room, which looks south over the Washington Monument. It was John F. Kennedy, however, who made the chair a glamorous must-have. Kennedy suffered from chronic back pain, and his doctor suggested that sitting in a rocking chair might ease his discomfort. It worked so well that when he became president, Kennedy bought fourteen rockers from P&P Chair, a small North Carolina company, and put them in the Oval Office, his White House bedroom, Camp David, his summer home at Hyannis Port—even on Air Force One. The Hyannisport chair sold at Sotheby's for more than $400,000 in the mid-1990s.

While many people think of wooden rockers as rustic design, mid-century designers experimented with materials to give the chair a bit of an edge. Perhaps the most famous (and coveted) version is the molded plastic rocker created in 1948 by the famous mid-century furniture designing couple Charles and Ray Eames. American furniture manufacturing firm Herman Miller holds the license to the chairs, and since 1955 every employee welcoming a baby into their home has been offered an Eames rocker (worth on average $700 or more) or a savings bond. More than 90 percent have chosen the rocker. Wouldn't you?

Rose

Throughout history, no other bloom has been as revered and loved as the rose. The Greek poet Sappho called it "the queen of flowers," and since the days of the ancient Egyptians, its intoxicating scent and image have enchanted royalty, poets, and common folk alike.

At one of the many banquets that Cleopatra organized to captivate and delight her lover, Marc Antony, she had a hall filled 2 feet [61 cm] deep with rose petals. Cleopatra knew her audience; the Romans were utterly obsessed with roses. Entire towns in Italy were dedicated to supplying the blossoms to the Roman markets. The Greeks had discovered how to coax the flowers to bloom early by sprinkling them with warm water as soon as buds began to appear. Roman growers took this trick to another level, forcing roses to bloom year-round by growing the bushes among hot water pipes.

The demand for the flower in ancient Rome was so insatiable that cultural critic and poet Horace worried that obsessed growers would neglect their vineyards and olive groves. Romans threw roses at victory parades, decorated their villas with cut flowers, used the petals to stuff pillows, and wore garlands of the blossoms in their hair. Wealthy Romans would dine while lounging on a bed of petals and put them in their wine; suppertime was known as the "Hour of Rose." If a rose was suspended above the table, it was acknowledged that conversations made *sub rosa* (under the rose) during the meal would remain confidential. There was even a festival, Rosalia, dedicated to celebrating the flower.

Roses continued to attract European nobility and the well-to-do long after the fall of the Roman Empire. Louis XIV, the seventeenth-century luxury-loving Sun King, had servants whose sole responsibility was to perfume his rooms with rosewater and marjoram. Marie-Antoinette adored the flower. Perhaps it evoked fond memories. While traveling from Vienna to Versailles to marry Louis-Auguste, the fifteen-year-old spent the night in the town of Nancy, France. To calm her nerves, she slept on a bed of fresh petals of *Rosa gallica*, the French rose.

In her numerous redecoration projects at Versailles, she always managed to slip in a rose motif.

In England, birthplace of Shakespeare's "rose by any other name," the Wars of the Roses established a new royal dynasty when two families, the Yorks and the Lancasters, battled for the throne. The Yorkists used the white rose as their symbol; the Lancastrians chose the red. The end of the war came at Bosworth Field, where Richard III was defeated by Henry Tudor. Tudor became Henry VII and adopted the Tudor rose as his emblem, which was a marriage of the red rose of the Lancasters and the white rose of the Yorks.

One of the greatest admirers of the genus *Rosa* was Emperor Napoleon's wife, Josephine. Named Marie Josèphe-Rose Tascher de La Pagerie at birth, she was called Rose by her family. Napoleon insisted that she change her name, but even he couldn't squash her overwhelming passion for her namesake. Josephine spent a fortune on her rose garden at their château Malmaison, which contained more than two hundred varieties of the flower. She even commissioned portraits of her favorite blooms. Those pictures were the perfect advertisement. Combined with her influence and infectious passion, the images propelled France to the position of the world's largest producer of roses during the eighteenth and nineteenth centuries. A variety with a deep pink ruffled bloom, large petals, and a heady scent was named 'Empress Josephine' shortly after her death in 1814.

Maximalist decorator Dorothy Draper took the rose to the American masses in the 1930s. Inspired by Georgia O'Keeffe's celebrated flower paintings, she designed a fabric emblazoned with oversize cabbage roses for acclaimed fabric supplier F. Schumacher & Co. The bold style spoke to a public looking for something cheery, and soon the company produced over a million yards. It remains one of the company's all-time bestsellers.

In 1941, a Los Angeles ceramics company, Franciscan China, responded to the public passion for the flower with a line of earthen dinnerware decorated with a pink rose and a smattering of foliage. The pattern, Desert Rose, became one of the most popular American dinnerware patterns ever. More than sixty million pieces were sold between 1941 and 1964.

The rose is, by a wide margin, the most favored flower for both gardens and decor, and its image decorates everything from pillows to sheets to wallpaper to porcelain; its scent is a candle and diffuser favorite. It's hard to imagine another bloom with such passionate fans or a more distinguished history.

Shower

Who needs a bathtub when you can luxuriate in a massaging cascade of water that's set to your personal temperature preference and accompanied by your favorite music?

> **"Are you a bath person or a shower person? It is impossible to exaggerate the character-revealing difference between the two."**
>
> *—MICHEL TOURNIER,*
> LE MIROIR DES IDÉES, *1994*

But showers weren't always so sybaritic. The Greeks believed strongly in the moral superiority of the cold, no-nonsense rinse. Regular physical activity was an essential component of Greek masculinity and was always done in the nude (*gymnasium* means "naked place"). Prior to exercising, men oiled their bodies and covered themselves in a layer of sand to prevent getting chilled. After exercise, they scraped off the oil, sand, and sweat with a curved metal tool called a *strigil*. Then they stood under cold water poured through boar- and lion-faced spouts by a servant or slave standing on the other side of the wall.

The pleasure-loving Romans appreciated cleanliness as much as the Greeks—but once they replaced the cold shower with the sensuous pleasures of a warm bath, the rest of the world followed suit. That is, until between 1500 and 1700, when fear of disease put a halt to any form of bathing—shower, bath, or otherwise—and a change of linen undergarments was considered the safest way to get clean.

The collective cultural fear of water abated with the dawn of the Enlightenment, and a new understanding of the relationship between cleanliness and illness. People began to experiment with various methods of getting clean. Slowly the shower made its way back into society. So slowly, in fact, that in the summer of 1798, when Philadelphia Quaker Henry Drinker installed a shower in his backyard, his wife, Elizabeth, spent months warily watching her three daughters and the women servants, dressed in gowns and oil cloth caps, enter the wooden shower stall. Finally, the next July, she gave it a try. "I bore it better than I expected," she wrote in her diary, "not having been wett all over at once, for 28 years past."

The most intrepid explorers of the shower were the Victorians, who, aspiring to be like the great Greek thinkers, believed the colder, the better. British historian Edward Gibbon, author of *The Rise and Fall of the Roman Empire*, postulated that the licentious practice of bathing in warm water had brought about the destruction of Rome. Being able to endure a cold shower was considered a badge of superior morality and proof of maleness. (It's a sentiment with lasting influence, as evidenced by the modern German expression for a wimp—*Warmduscher*, or warm-showerer.) But not every Victorian unequivocally embraced the character test of a pounding cold shower. Mary Anne Disraeli, the nineteenth-century British prime minister's wife, quipped that her husband had infinite morals, but no physical courage: she always had to pull the shower operating chain for him.

I DO MY BEST THINKING IN THE SHOWER

· · · · · · · · · · · ·

While taking a shower in his Munich hotel bathroom, NASA engineer Jim Crocker reached up to adjust the shower-head, noticed that it was mounted on adjustable sliding rods, and realized that a similar setup might just be able to fix the damaged mirror that had knocked the Hubble Space Telescope out of commission. Thanks to that German shower-head, the Hubble telescope is still sending images of space back to Earth.

The transformation of the shower from a feared instrument of torture to the pièce de résistance of the bathroom can be credited to Boston's Tremont House. When the luxury hotel opened in 1829, it was the first to feature a lobby, bellboys, and individually lockable rooms. It was also the first to feature indoor plumbing, and offered guests the first dedicated rooms for bathing—eight on the basement floor. Not exactly luxury by modern standards, considering there were 170 rooms, but certainly a step up from a basin and pitcher. Despite the inevitable lines for the bathroom, the hotel was an immediate success. Because of the Tremont, the shower became the preferred way for on-the-go travelers to clean up,

BATHROOM DE LUXE

• • • • • • • • • • • •

American designer Elsie de Wolfe deserves credit (or blame, depending on your perspective) for turning the bathroom into the over-the-top destination it is today. In the early 1920s, she was known for combining modern fixtures with extravagant details, as in wealthy socialite Mai Coe's bathroom in Oyster Bay, New York. The violet marble sink matched the marble base of the shower, which featured gold-plated hardware (tarnished for an antique effect). The makeup table was painted with floral swags and paired with a stool upholstered in needlepoint. The room was lit by a crystal chandelier. Six silver pedestals, on which color-coordinated live cockatoos would perch, added a bit of dramatic flair. This inspired design helped start the craze of elegantly appointed bathrooms that were decorated as part of the house, rather than sterile, functional spaces.

plumbed for hot water and connected to city sewer systems. This meant that having hot water in the home was not a luxury but an expectation. Wartime technological advances like ventilation fans also found a new audience in the home market. It was the beginning of innovations in the bathroom that we take for granted today, like glass enclosures, the fogless mirror, in-floor heating, and multiple showerheads with programmable sensors.

The shower has become the centerpiece of the bathroom. Whether all this obsessing over warm (or even better, hot!) water showers is a sign of the weakening of society and a repeat of the Fall of Rome, as the Victorians suggested, is for the future to decide.

thanks to its speed and efficiency. Once hotel guests had experienced a bit of bathroom luxury, they wanted to find a way to bring it home.

In the early 1900s, bathrooms became more space efficient when an overhead shower was incorporated into the bathtub. After World War II, as home building exploded, new neighborhoods were

Sofa

We may spend a third of our lives in bed—but when we're awake at a home, we are more than likely sitting (or lying) on the sofa.

> **"There are only two things of real importance in a woman's life . . . her bed and her sofa."**
>
> —*DIANA VREELAND*

The comfy upholstered sofa we know and love had its origins in France. During the turbulent Middle Ages, kings, queens, and nobles would travel from castle to castle on diplomatic missions with all their furniture in tow: chests (for luggage and seating), trestle tables, beds, and stools. Portability, not comfort, was the selling point.

This was the status quo until ten-year-old Louis XIV had to flee Paris to escape the threat of a civil war in 1648. There hadn't been time to move the royal furniture, so when the young king and his courtiers arrived at the palace in Saint-Germain-en-Laye, they found it completely empty. Members of the royal entourage were forced to spend the night on piles of straw. The aristocracy wasn't known for their flexibility, and the young king was humiliated by their complaining. He spent the rest of his life compensating by creating a magnificent home at Versailles.

The first step in realizing his vision was to create a sustainable French furniture industry. One of the major players was Gobelins Manufactory. Originally a small tapestry manufacturer, they began adding padding to the seats, backs, and arms of chairs and covering the cushioning with their fabric, which was nailed to the frame. What the king initiated his courtiers imitated, and soon the wealthy and powerful throughout France were clamoring for more upholstered pieces. Upholstered chairs grew larger and larger until two

WHAT TO CALL IT?

· · · · · · · · · · · ·

The word "sofa," derived from the Arabic word for wool, Ṣuffa, was first used in France at the end of the seventeenth century. Nathan Bailey's Dictionarium Britannicum *(1736) referred to its Turkish ancestor, the divan, a long mattress placed on the floor and against a wall with a cushion to lean against. Bailey defined it as a "sort of alcove much used in Asia . . . it is an apartment of state . . . furnished with rich carpets and cushions." At this time, the word began to appear in common usage in its accepted sense in England. Although interchangeable in American English, a couch is technically a sofa without a back, and is also called a chaise or daybed.*

people could fit comfortably on one. That two-seater (basically a love seat) was, in effect, the world's first sofa.

The lure of comfort made this new form of seating difficult to resist, especially because, at the time, sitting down was a matter of protocol, not comfort. There was a lot of standing around. At Versailles, only a select few were allowed to be seated in the presence of the royal family. Just four years after the sofa arrived at court, the king's sister-in-law wrote her German cousins, "All the men now sit down in the pres-

ence of M. the Dauphin and Madame the Duchesse de Bourgogne; some of them are even stretched out full-length on sofas . . . You can't imagine what it's like here because it no longer looks like a court."

Behavior was not the only thing that changed. Clothing also transformed to better accommodate the new furniture, becoming lighter and less formal. Heavy fabrics and stiff boning in bodices were out. Light silks and newly imported Indian cottons much better suited to reclining were in. And as the furniture and clothing changed, so did behavior. It's hard to be formal when you're sprawled on a couch with one leg slung over the arm.

Between 1675 and 1740, people went from living with back-torturing seats to being surrounded by a plethora of comfortable choices. To entice repeat buyers, manufacturers made each model more luxurious than the last. Looking to expand their market, French manufacturers used engravings of famously beautiful noblewomen draped over the cushions to advertise their products. (Sex always sells.) French novelists featured a sofa, rather than the bed, as the scene of a seduction, as in the 1735 novel *Le Paysan Parvenu (The Fortunate Peasant)*. It had such a provocative reputation that even as late as the 1780s, the English would swap out their sofas for stiff wooden chairs when important visitors came to call.

Comfort triumphed over propriety, though, and all of Europe was infected by sofa mania. "Today," wrote Voltaire, "social behavior is easier than in the past . . . ladies can be seen reading on sofas or daybeds without causing embarrassment to their friends and acquaintances." The social acceptability of the sofa was sealed when Catherine the Great of Russia received her ambassadors while lying on one. By the nineteenth century, they were found in every room of the house, including bedrooms, dining rooms—even bathrooms.

There may be no other single piece of furniture with the power to transform the mood of a space—and sometimes even a person. As British decorator Elsie de Wolfe wrote in her 1913 decorating manual, *A House in Good Taste*, "I have seen a shy young woman completely changed because she happened to sit upon a certain deep cushioned sofa of rose-colored damask." Whether it's a classic overstuffed piece or a low-slung modern design, the sofa today commands the place of honor in our living spaces.

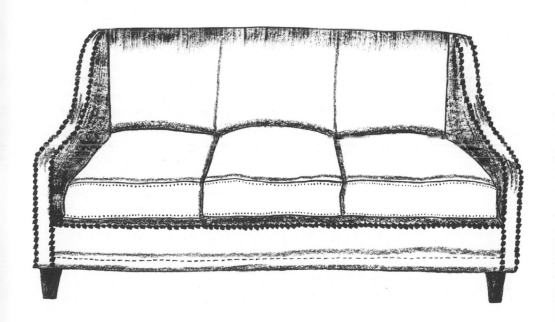

Spoon

The spoon is the first utensil most of us encounter as infants. It's also probably the first eating utensil humans created. As British food writer Bee Wilson has pointed out, "There are fork cultures and there are chopstick cultures: but all the peoples of the world use spoons."

Until the seventeenth century, leaving home without your spoon would have been almost as unthinkable as forgetting your smartphone is today. And what the utensil was made of would have said as much about your social standing as the jewels (or lack of them) on your fingers. (If you were really *someone*, your spoon would be just as bejeweled as your fingers.)

The earliest spoons were made of whatever was available: a shell tied to a stick, a curved piece of horn, a carved piece of wood. Skilled craftsmen later made wooden spoons things of beauty. Ancient Persians used pear wood to fabricate large yet improbably delicate drinking spoons. The long handle was intricately incised with lacework and the bowl was almost paper-thin. In seventeenth-century Wales, a suitor gave a wooden love spoon to the object of his affection to demonstrate his ability to provide for a family. The more complex the design, the better the provider. Sometimes secret messages were hidden in the carvings.

In the Middle Ages, silver spoons were popular baptismal gifts. It didn't hurt that they were the least expensive item of silver that you could give. It's from this custom that we get the expression "born with a silver spoon in

LITTLE, BIG

● ● ● ● ● ● ● ● ● ● ● ●

Only two spoons from the Victorian table have remained a part of the modern flatware set. The tablespoon, named to distinguish it from a cooking spoon that remained in the kitchen, was brought to the table. The teaspoon, sized to fit into a teacup, was created in the eighteenth century to dole out precious imported tea.

his mouth." (Those with less disposable income might give spoons made from less expensive materials, like horn or wood.)

> ## "They dined on mince, and slices of quince, / Which they ate with a runcible spoon; / And hand in hand, on the edge of the sand, / They danced by the light of the moon."
>
> —EDWARD LEAR,
> "THE OWL AND THE PUSSYCAT"

Of course, the spoon also had to be made in the latest fashion. This meant the handle was finished with a finial top and either set with a jewel or cast as an elaborate figure. If you wanted to impress the new parents with your generosity, you would gift the new baby with an apostle spoon. The finial would be in the likeness of the apostle for whom the child was named, or the local saint. Wealthy godparents might give a set of thirteen spoons (one for each of the twelve apostles, and one for Jesus). Those with smaller (yet still robust) bank accounts might gift a set of six.

As clothing fashions changed, so did the styles for spoons. In the seventeenth century, the prevailing style of large, elaborate lace ruffs and collars caused spoon handles to be elongated to help protect expensive garments from spillage. Ornamental finial handles were out. Long, wide, flat handles with plenty of space for engraving were in. To accommodate the elaborate patterns, the grip was so wide that people clutched their spoons in their fists, rather than with their fingers as we do today.

By the eighteenth century, you no longer needed to bring your own spoon to dinner. Now the pressure of having a stylish spoon fell to the host. This was nothing compared to the crushing burden later felt by nineteenth-century hostesses, who had to choose the correct spoon to serve with each dish. An anxiety over touching food, coupled with the newly invented technique of silver plating, made it now possible (and desirable) to create a spoon for every occasion. Spoons were made in every shape and size for nearly every purpose and course: iced beverage spoons, egg spoons (often gilded to prevent oxidation by the yolk), ice cream spoons, bouillon (a clear soup) spoons, after-dinner coffee spoons, chocolate spoons, salt spoons—even a mustache spoon with a shaped ledge to keep the mustache out of soup's way. (As for the spoon "that dished out mince and slices of quince"? While the runcible spoon is now known as the spork, at the time Lear wrote that fabled poem it was merely his favorite nonsense word.)

Luckily for the decision weary, modern life (and the lack of servants) has drastically reduced the number of spoons required at a meal. Unless you're invited to a very formal dinner, most of us only have to choose between a teaspoon and a tablespoon. Cue the collective sigh of relief.

THE TASTIEST SPOON

....

The prophet Nathan used a gold spoon to anoint Solomon, the king of Israel. For President Martin Van Buren, a golden spoon would be his downfall. When the public learned that Van Buren was using golden spoons in the middle of a major recession, his 1848 reelection campaign never recovered. (Never mind that the gold-plated spoons had actually been purchased by James Monroe, and Van Buren was actually so frugal he would not even make necessary repairs to the White House.) William Henry Harrison won the election.

But President Monroe may have been on to something. According to recent scientific research, what your spoon is made of may actually affect the taste of your food. London-based researcher Zoe Laughlin had subjects eat yogurt from spoons made of seven different metals: copper, gold, silver, tin, zinc, chrome, and stainless steel. The winner? Gold. Laughlin said: "The gold spoon is just sort of divine . . . it makes everything you eat seem more delicious."

Tablecloth

Even in these days of machine-washable, mass-produced textiles, we can (often) gauge the tone of an occasion by the kind of cloth (or lack of it) on the table. Vintage chintz sheets say a bridal shower tea; burlap runners over undyed linen signal a rustic country wedding; checked oilcloth is a classic look for a backyard barbecue. Floor-length white, and you're probably looking at the kind of fancy restaurant that uses a crumb sweep between courses.

Medieval diners would be horrified at our casual attitude toward table linens. For knights and their ladies, good linen was a sign of good breeding. Eating on a bare table was for the peasants. If you could afford it (and maybe even if you couldn't), your table would be covered by a white cloth and pleated for a little extra finesse. A colored tablecloth was thought to impair the appetite. (The exception to the white-only rule: In rural areas, the top cloth might be woven with colorful stripes, plaids, or checks.) Diners only sat along one side of the table, where the tablecloth hung to the floor to protect guests from drafts and keep the animals from walking over their feet.

The medieval white tablecloths were commonly made from damask, a cloth woven with a geometric pattern. The material came to Europe from Damascus, Syria, with the Crusaders. Damask could be woven from velvet or silk—but it was linen damask, with its brilliant sheen and whiteness, that conquered the table. (An added virtue: It was washable.) But for all damask's charms, it wasn't inexpensive, and sometimes even kings had to economize: Louis XV of France had white tablecloths made of cotton embroidered to resemble damask.

Whatever the material, the fabric would be purchased in great lengths and then cut to measure as needed. The lady of the castle would do a careful inventory of the linen and give each tablecloth a grade; the best was reserved for the head table, second best for the second-best table, and so on. Linens had a fairly long life, and the best tablecloths worked their way down the social scale until they ended their life polishing silver.

Before indoor plumbing, you couldn't throw your tablecloths in the washer and dryer. So when things began to get a little messy, the cloth was simply flipped over. The condition of the cloth at your place could also indicate whether or not you were in favor at court. A knight could be dishonored by setting his place on the soiled side of the cloth. If an even harsher punishment was needed, the tablecloth was cut through to his left and right,

signifying that he was no longer part of the brotherhood.

A couple of hundred years later, during the Renaissance, your social status could be cemented by the caliber of your dinner parties. The wealthiest Renaissance households had a full-time party planner on staff, called the *scalco*. He (and it was always a he) was responsible for everything from the location to the party favors. He was also in charge of one of the most important rituals of the Renaissance feast: the layering of tablecloths. For most parties, whether it was a middle-class meal of three courses or a high-society soiree of eighteen, there would be three table coverings: one that the guests sat down to on arrival, one revealed midway through the dinner, and one for the dessert course (with a layer of leather between the cloths to prevent any stains from seeping through). In 1529, a party given by Cardinal Ippolito d'Este in honor of his brother's recent marriage upped the ante. After the fruit course (usually the last of a nine-course meal), the third tablecloth was removed, revealing two more linens and another nine courses on the way.

Such refinement took a bit longer to make it across the ocean to the New World, where diners often didn't distinguish between the table covering and the napkin. In George Washington's 1750 book *The Rules of Civility*, he urged his fellow colonists to refrain from using the tablecloth to clean their

MAGIC TRICK

· · · · · · · · · · · · ·

Charlemagne, ninth-century Holy Roman emperor, used his tablecloth as part of a party trick. After the meal, he would throw his asbestos tablecloth into the fire so that all the crumbs would burn away, leaving it perfectly clean and ready for the next feast.

faces. Even a century later, foreign visitors to America were appalled by the American preference for using the tablecloth to wipe their mouths.

By the time of Queen Victoria's reign, the dining table had become a show-piece, crafted of fine woods like mahogany. The tablecloth protected the beautiful surface underneath. After the main meal, servants would remove the white tablecloth to show-case the gleaming polished table. This was the signal that the focus of the dinner had changed from eating to drinking. Once the wood itself became something to highlight, the appearance of a white linen tablecloth began to dwindle.

Precisely because it's not necessary, a tablecloth has a way of slowing down the meal, reminding us that time with family and friends is always a special occasion.

Tassel

Your first encounter with a tassel may have been on the mortarboard at your high school graduation. Maybe a pair adorned your loafers or decorated a handbag. Or perhaps you visited a luxe hotel and found a silken tassel hanging from an armoire door or a curtain tie.

A tassel is simply a tuft of thread, cord, or other material hanging from a knot at one end. Originally a technique to prevent textiles from unraveling, they are also an easy way to embellish a garment, woven belt, or jewelry.

Whether bright and big or small and discreet, the tassel is a design element with an impressive pedigree. It is, in fact, mentioned in the Bible: The Lord commands Moses to teach the Israelites how to make them. Tassels also play an important role in Eastern religions: Paper versions were used by Shinto priests in ancient Japan to ward off evil spirits. Muslims and Hindus use them on religious beads, and Buddhist meditation beads are tied with them.

The Chinese incorporated tassels into their silk clothing. When the emperor's subjects approached him, they held the silk tassels on their court robes in their hands to assure him that their voluminous sleeves concealed no weapons. Then, in 540 C.E., the Roman emperor Justinian and two Persian monks successfully smuggled silkworms from China, primarily motivated by the desire to make the embellishment more available to Western aristocrats. In the process, they bypassed the Silk Road and started the Byzantine silk industry, which would keep all of Europe in the fabric until the Middle Ages.

The tassel moved from wearable to hangable thanks to those arbiters of all things stylish, the French. In France, the art of making the decorations was serious business; apprentices trained for seven years just to become masters. The new French versions contained more than three hundred silk, gold, or silver threads each. It could take as many as nine hundred hours to make a single one, and it was all done by hand. At a time when any upholstery was an extravagance, the tassel was an ostentatious indulgence. Just as a perfectly placed diamond was the finishing touch for a certain set of high society, the artfully appointed ornament gave a certain je ne sais quoi to the à la mode furniture of the day, such as heavily upholstered beds and plush cushions.

Tassels were so central to privileged living that they even played a role in a mystery at Versailles. Louis XIV's state bed—including the headboard and bed curtains—was decorated with oversized tassels of ostrich and heron feathers woven with heavy gold and silver thread and accented with gold thread flowers. The tassels proved to be a little too tempting, and a thief managed to cut off all of them. That night at dinner,

just as the dessert course was about to be served, someone flung a large package onto the table directly in front of the king. There was immediate panic from the servants, but the king merely cocked his head and said, "I think these are my tassels." The culprit (and the reason for both the theft and the quick return) was never found.

As usual, once the French deemed tassels cool, the rest of Europe followed suit. Their availability was aided by the fact that much of their manufacturing was done by French Huguenots (a Protestant sect). Fleeing France and Catholic persecution in the seventeenth century, they took their expertise to more tolerant countries like England and the Netherlands.

Tassel mania continued unabated. For the growing merchant class in the nineteenth century, the completely frivolous and flamboyant accessory was the perfect way to flaunt their newly acquired wealth. Tassels adorned almost everything from horses and carriages to cushions, curtains, and keys. Napoleon used lavish golden versions on his throne and in his bed-rooms. The Victorians, who had a love of embellishment and little sense of restraint, went completely gaga for the silken ornaments. "The Victorians loved covering up everything with little mats, generally decorated with flimsy tas-sels . . . care apparently being taken to select a material which might be relied

TASSEL CALCULATOR

∙∙∙∙∙∙∙∙∙∙∙∙∙

In the Ryukyu Islands off the southwest coast of Japan, men traditionally used tassels on their belts as calculators. Threads were divided between their fingers to keep track of the total count (for example, the "ones" are held between the thumb and forefinger; "tens" between the forefinger and middle finger).

upon to attract the greatest quantity of dust," wrote Ralph Nevill in his 1930 book, *The Gay Victorians.*

Eventually people tired of fussy, over-decorated furnishings, and by the early twentieth century, a preference for unadorned, cleaner silhouettes had taken hold. But the use of tassels never completely disappeared, and they remained an important cultural and artistic adornment in rural cultures throughout the world. In the 1960s, Peace Corps workers returned from their assignments abroad, bringing home Afghan, African, Asian, and Arabian folk tassels. Soon, import and counterculture shops began selling these artifacts and revived the appetite of home decorators.

Teapot

Legend has it that the first cup of tea was drunk by the Chinese emperor Shennong, a mythical ruler in prehistoric China. That first cuppa was the result of an accident—dried leaves of *Camellia sinensis* (the shrub from which all Chinese teas are made) serendipitously fell into a pot of boiling water.

> ## "[T]here are few hours in life more agreeable than the hour dedicated to the ceremony known as afternoon tea."
>
> —HENRY JAMES, THE PORTRAIT OF A LADY, *1881*

First brewed in individual cups by whisking leaves in hot water, tea was made in a single-serving pot by the thirteenth century. The infusion was sipped directly from the spout. By the sixteenth century, multi-serving pots with handles and spouts were the teatime implement of choice.

Europe was introduced to tea and teapots by the East India Company. The British importers dominated the Eastern trade routes, and during the

LATE TO THE TEA PARTY

• • • • • • • • • • • •

While the British may have brought tea to Europe, it took foreign royalty to make it the beverage of choice in the Isles. When the Portuguese princess Catherine of Braganza arrived in England in the mid–seventeenth century, the first thing the future wife of King Charles II asked for was a cup of tea. She was promptly handed, instead, a cup of ale. Luckily, Catherine had stashed a large supply of her favorite beverage in her luggage. Soon green tea, without milk or sugar, became all the rage in the English court.

seventeenth century began importing teapots from China. They were stored in the lower portion of cargo ships as ballast to improve stability. The tea was kept dry above the waterline. A shipment of tea could take a year to travel from China to Europe, so it was used sparingly. It was brewed by pouring boiling water from the pot directly over leaves set in tiny porcelain bowls.

In France, tea caught on quickly. In fact, it was *because* of all its accoutrements that the French nobility embraced teatime. The Sun King, Louis XIV, became a fervent consumer only after receiving a solid gold teacup as a gift from the king of Siam.

The first seventeenth-century European teapots made specially for brewing tea were crafted from metals like silver. Clay pottery couldn't withstand high water temperatures, and the secrets of porcelain manufacturing eluded much of Europe until the eighteenth century. The spherical teapot that we are familiar with today first appeared on tables in France in 1720, and soon spread throughout the continent and across the English Channel.

In Germany and France, porcelain manufacture was a kingly venture. There was more of an entrepreneurial spirit in England, and keeping the country stocked with teapots made the immense fortunes of eighteenth-century tycoons like Josiah Wedgwood and Josiah Spode. Their factories created fanciful teapots fashioned to look like a head of cauliflower or the

A LITTLE BIRDIE TOLD ME

· · · · · · · · · · · · ·

Michael Graves is one of the most iconic architects of the twentieth century, with numerous awards and accolades to his name. Despite this success, he's best known for a teakettle. More than thirty years ago, Graves was asked to design a tea set for Alessi, the nearly hundred-year-old Italian housewares company. The silver kettle has the simple architectural shape of a gently sloping inverted cone—but it wasn't the shape that made it stand out. It was the bird-shaped whistle in the spout that sounded the boiling water alarm. The little bird was a nod to the morning crows of roosters from Graves's Indiana childhood, and it caught the fancy of consumers. It is Alessi's all-time bestselling item. In true design democracy fashion, the Italian-made object was reimagined for Target as a $25 version. The bird whistle kettle (1.3 million of them) flew off the shelves and remains one of the most sought-after kettles in the world.

ceramics found in Roman ruins. But the biggest boost to the British teapot industry wasn't innovative design: By the end of the eighteenth century, shrinking profit margins compelled the British East India Company to stop importing porcelain. That was like a winning lottery ticket for the British ceramics industry.

Even in our modern world of tea bags, a simple teapot remains a kitchen essential for the true tea lover. To aid in the quest for the perfect cup, there are tea ateliers in nearly every major city to match the teapot with the brew. (Teas needing short infusion times can be brewed in flat pots, while pear-, bell-, or bowl-shaped ones are good for longer steeps.) The more serious your tea obsession becomes, the more tea essentials you may find yourself accumulating. In 2011, a man in China made the *Guinness Book of World Records* with his collection of thirty thousand teapots.

Tented Room

A tented room is the adult (and chic) version of a blanket fort. Using fabric as wall decor began in the Middle Ages as a way to insulate interiors. What started out as a practical way to take the chill off stone castle walls became a luxe way to decorate by utilizing sumptuous textiles and tapestries.

Draping material to evoke the inside of a tent was the brainchild of the eighteenth-century French it-girl, Empress Josephine, wife of Napoleon Bonaparte. The couple had gone shopping for a country house just before Napoleon left on his Egyptian campaign and Josephine fell in love with the Château de Malmaison (French for "bad house") the moment she stepped onto the property. Napoleon didn't quite get her vision for the dilapidated country estate, which was located ten miles west of Paris. He declared its name accurate and buying the house entirely out of the question. But the moment he left for Egypt in 1799, Josephine borrowed the money, bought the house, and set about transforming it.

She enlisted the help of Charles Percier and Pierre Fontaine, France's most

fashionable interior designers, to make her diamond in the rough sparkle. The pair took an entirely new approach: They draped material over doors and swagged it along the walls all the way to the ceiling, creating drooping curves of fabric in solid silks or striped cotton with tasseled or fringe borders. Tented rooms were sprinkled throughout the buildings, including the bedrooms, entryway—even Napoleon's Council Room.

The flamboyantly luxurious hangings were meant to reference Napoleon's forays into the Middle East. Ever susceptible to flattery, Napoleon appreciated the appeal to his ego, but he didn't exactly warm to the look. He was known to call the vestibule used by the domestic staff "a fairground tent fit only for showing animals." Despite Napoleon's opinion of their taste, Percier and Fontaine published catalogs featuring the interiors at Malmaison, and the style quickly became famous. Throughout the eighteenth century, it was copied in Europe and America, evoking a romanticized vision of Egyptian and Turkish design.

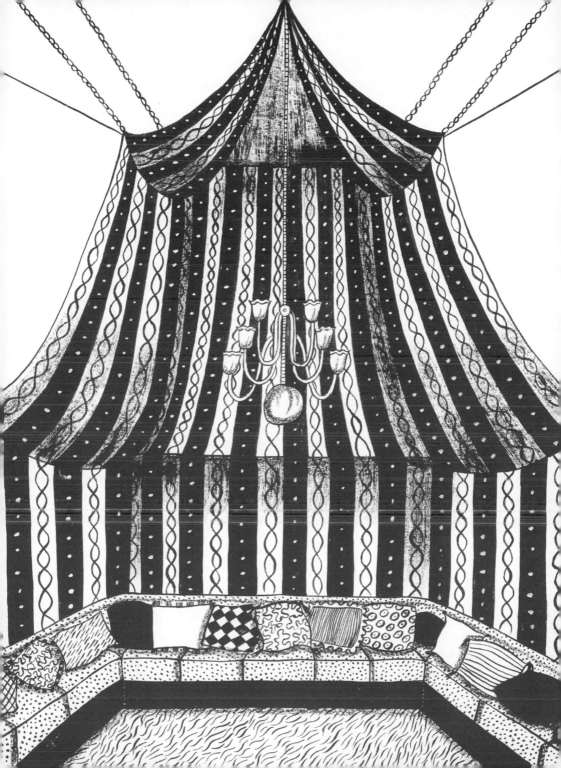

One hundred and thirty years later, American tobacco heiress Doris Duke circled the globe looking for unique travel experiences. Dubbed "the world's richest girl," she spent her honeymoon traveling through North Africa, the Middle East, and India. In 1935, inspired by the architecture of buildings like India's Taj Mahal and Iran's Chehel Sotoun, Duke built a mansion in Honolulu she called Shangri La. She had become enamored of the elaborate tents she had seen in her travels, and wanted to re-create the experience at home. Designed to evoke a royal Middle Eastern pavilion, her dining room was draped floor to ceiling with 453 yards [414 m] of striped green and blue cotton fabric that had been custom made in India. The fabric cascaded down every inch of wall space and was cinched at the ceiling. A large crystal chandelier hung in the center above a low dining table. The room created a sensation when it appeared in *Vogue* magazine in the 1960s.

Duke wasn't alone in her passion for the exotic. The fashion for all things Eastern became the epitome of high style, in part inspired by the Beatles' embrace of the aesthetic. Tented rooms were again all the rage. The 1960s interpretation was bohemian in spirit, with bright colors and Indian- and Middle Eastern–inspired patterns rather than the more sedate stripes or solids favored by Empress Josephine. Jackie Kennedy's sister, the soigné Lee Radziwill, had a tented room designed for her by Renzo Mongiardino, the Italian design guru for the international jet set of the twentieth century. Mongiardino took Indian printed cottons with flower and paisley patterns in similar color families—blue, yellow, red, and ivory—sliced them apart, and recombined them in a patchwork effect. The room was photographed for *Vogue* in 1966.

In an effort to make tented rooms more broadly accessible, Angelo Donghia, design magazine superstar and one of the most influential designers of the latter half of the twentieth century, partnered with Ira Seret, who had a design shop in Santa Fe. They created an interpretation of an Afghan wedding tent featuring boldly patterned, hand-appliquéd fabric, ready-made to be pitched in a room. It was a huge hit, and Donghia's own fabric-draped living room was featured in *Vogue* in 1971. In the ultimate trickle-down effect, the style became adopted in dorm rooms and hippie communes across the country. It was a cheap way to decorate, even on a student budget.

A tented room, filled with sensuous color and pattern, is like an escape to another place and time. The bohemian look is not for the demure, though. But for those who wish to create a fairy-tale retreat within their home, nothing can compete with a dramatically draped room.

Tile

Although we think of tile as a solution for keeping our bathrooms, kitchens, and floors functional and easy to clean, it has an ancient history as a decorative element used for thousands of years. The earliest known tiles are Egyptian, and date from 4000 B.C.E. They were also used on interior (and sometimes exterior) walls, floors, and ceilings by the Assyrians and Babylonians, and throughout the Islamic Empire.

In ancient Greece, tile floor art was an essential part of a well-decorated room. And for a style maven of the second century B.C.E., there was no floor treatment quite as chic as a mosaic. Using tiny pieces of marble, terra-cotta, glass, and sometimes even gold inset into the ground with cement, skilled artists created exquisite pieces of art on both floors and walls. The best of the best was Sosu, whose most showstopping work was called "unswept floor." It depicted pieces of fruit, fish, and other foods and rubbish as if they had fallen from the dining table. His wall mosaic of a group of doves drinking from a bowl of water was said to be so realistic that real

doves flew into it, trying to join their stone brethren.

The Romans were equally enamored with the beauty of mosaic floors—so much so that Julius Caesar traveled in battle with a portable mosaic floor so that he could enjoy some of the luxury he had at home. The tile was applied to wooden planks that could be assembled and disassembled quickly.

The combination of functionality and beauty made tiles popular through the Middle Ages and into the Renaissance. The Alhambra Palace in Granada, Spain, was famous for its mosaics, decorated with stunningly intricate geometric patterns. (These same tiles would later inspire Dutch graphic artist M.C. Escher to create the repeating patterns in his own work.) Originally a Moorish fortress and palace, Alhambra became the seat of the royal court of Ferdinand and Isabella. When Christopher Columbus went to the Alhambra to ask the royal couple to fund his expedition, he walked through the tile-covered corridors of the monumental Hall of Ambassadors.

In most Renaissance buildings, tiles were mainly used on the floors. One notable exception was the extravagant getaway built by Louis XIV in 1670 to celebrate his passion for his mistress, the Marquise de Montespan. It sat at one end of Versailles's Grand Canal and was inspired by the marquise's taste for luxury. The king commissioned an exotic pavilion the likes of which Europe had never seen: Its roof was covered in thousands of sparkling ceramic tiles in the style of "blue and white" Ming china. Entering the Trianon de Porcelaine was like walking into a porcelain universe. Inside, tiles covered the floors. The white walls were swathed with tile-inspired cobalt blue motifs; furniture, painted to look as if it was tile-clad, filled the building. It was a fairytale castle for a storybook romance. In 1673, architectural historian André Félibien observed, "Everyone found the palace enchanting."

However captivating the love shack was, it also illustrates why ornamental tiles were usually confined to interior spaces in northern Europe. While further south, tiles decorate both the interior and the exterior of buildings, frost can do enormous damage to the fragile and porous material. Within twenty years, Louis's porcelain-clad structure was damaged beyond repair and had to be pulled down.

These days, perhaps the most iconic and widely used are the simple 3-by-6-inch [7.5-by-15-cm] tiles that line the walls of the New York City subway system. Now known as "subway tiles," the white rectangles were created in 1904 by architects George C. Heins and Christopher Grant La Farge for the City Hall subway station, New York City's first. They were both a hygienic solution and an aesthetic one: The luminous white reflected light, brightening the subterranean space, and could be embellished with decorative mosaics. Today, subway tiles come in a rainbow of colors, and are often used in kitchens and bathrooms.

Although it's rare to find exterior tile in a contemporary building, it can generally be found in every room of the house. Terra-cotta squares from Mexico make a cool footing for the kitchen floor. Handmade glazed ceramic tiles produced in California and geometrically patterned cement tiles from Morocco can add texture to a fireplace surround or backsplash. Glass tiles can turn an ordinary shower into a spa-like oasis. Some homeowners incorporate custom mosaic designs into entry halls. Wood-look flooring tiles can be used throughout the home. Colorful, versatile, and timeless, tiles bring the past into the present.

Tolix Marais A Chair

The name might not be familiar, but if you've ever lunched at a sidewalk cafe, chances are you've sat on a Tolix Marais A chair. Made from galvanized steel, the chair was designed and created in 1934 by celebrated furniture maker Xavier Pauchard. These days, the Tolix Marais A is the poster child for industrial chic. It pops up in kitchens, living rooms, and offices—it was even the desk chair of choice for *Vogue* editor-in-chief Anna Wintour. The design darling of lifestyle blogs throughout the world, it has earned a place in prestigious museum collections like those at Vitra Design, Museum of Modern Art, and the Centre Pompidou.

Designer Pauchard grew up in the mountainous Morvan region of France, far away from the glamorous urban centers that would eventually come to embrace his celebrated creations. He learned the family trade, roofing, from his father. Whether it was roofs, cookware, or toys, if it was made from tinplate (sheets of iron protected from corrosion by dipping them in molten tin), Pauchard and his father could

fabricate or fix it. They walked from town to town, announcing their arrival with a pan flute, signaling the locals to bring out their items for repair. While he walked and worked, Pauchard dreamed of opening his own workshop. There he would craft and sell products of his own design, made of a new, more rust-resistant material that had recently been invented: iron or steel, coated with zinc.

The metallurgic process that filled Pauchard's daydreams was called galvanization. In fourteenth-century India, it was used to protect steel armor. It was refined (and publicized) in France in 1742 by chemist Paul Jacques Malouin and Luigi Galvani, a pioneer in the field of electricity—but the technique took some time to catch on. It eventually gained widespread use in Britain and America in the nineteenth century, and Pauchard was the first in France to adopt it.

Following the illustrations in American technical manuals, Pauchard conducted his own experiments. Even though he began to feel the effects of zinc

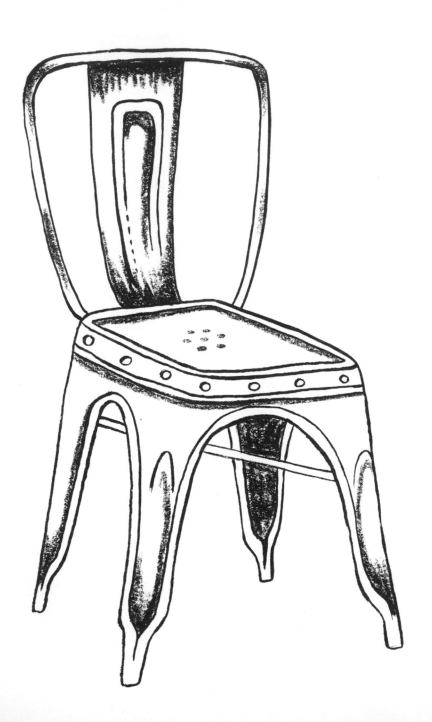

poisoning—numbness, weakness, and nausea—he continued working with the toxic metal until he felt confident enough in his understanding of the material to open his own workshop: Tolix. Initially, the factory made everything from toys to kitchen utensils. But it was the chairs that would have lasting resonance.

It's ironic that a chair that appears to be the embodiment of industrial design was—and still is—meticulously handcrafted. Pauchard hammered the sheet metal, carving out the shape of the chair, and then welded the pieces together. The Tolix Marais A looks so simple that it's hard to believe it takes a hundred manual steps to create each one, and that no two are ever exactly the same. The chairs were finished with a coat of paint, usually a bright red or a dark green, and intended to be a practical and long-lasting object. The holes in the seat are for rain drainage, allowing it to be used outside—a key component to its popularity, especially among bistro and café owners. Another bonus: its portability and small storage footprint. The chair can be stacked twenty-five high.

The Tolix Marais A was known as a solid (yet elegant) functional café chair until the 1990s, when the fashion for industrial chic took France by storm. A small group of antique dealers began collecting and selling furniture pieces otherwise destined for the scrap pile. Eager for something that felt fresh and authentic after decades of more formal antiques like the Louis XVI chair, homeowners embraced the rustic, unfinished look. Anything that had an industrial pedigree, from factory lights to metal wastepaper baskets, was snapped up by collectors. Dealers in New York City were quick to take note of the new trend and began selling similar roughed-up relics at high prices, creating a market for classic examples like the Tolix Marais A as well as new pieces.

We can thank English designer Terence Conran and Paul Hawken of the Smith & Hawken catalog for introducing the rest of the world to the Tolix Marais A in 1988. But it was in 1995, when Robert Redford's mail-order Sundance catalog featured the chair, that demand exploded. Now there are thousands of authentic Tolix chairs sold in the United States every year—each still handmade, using the same hundred-step process, in Autun, France, the Burgundy town where Tolix first began. Although knockoffs abound, they lack the sturdy weight of the originals. These days you can find the chairs in fifty different colors (or hunt down vintage ones in classic red or natural steel). Tolix also produces a stool and an armchair based on the same design.

From its humble beginnings, the Tolix Marais A has moved beyond cafés and bistros to grace nearly every room in the house. And if it's a good enough perch from which to launch the world's leading fashion magazine, then it just might be the right chair from which to propel your own dreams forward.

Topiary

Today, a good place to experience the classic Roman art of topiary is at Disneyland, where fantastical botanical sculptures have been delighting park goers since 1963. The word "topiary" comes from the Latin word *toparius*, which means "garden designer"; it's defined as the practice of shaping trees and shrubs into geometric or figurative forms. Walt Disney was inspired to add these living ornaments to his California theme park after visiting topiary gardens in Europe. Though the ostriches and elephants at Disneyland are impressive, they're simple in comparison to the elaborate work of the Roman artists, who created ornate installations featuring fleets of ships and armies for their Roman emperors.

After the fall of Rome, like so many aspects of ancient Roman culture, including making wine and bathing, the art of topiary was preserved in monasteries. There, monks designed simple hedge mazes that consisted of a single winding walkway, ideal for meditative strolling.

During the Renaissance, wealthy Italian families took inspiration from the monasteries and created elaborate topiary-filled gardens at their villas. The fad for these living sculptures soon spread throughout Europe. When King Louis XIV turned his grandfather's hunting lodge into the magnificent Palace of Versailles, he commissioned André Le Nôtre to design an ornate formal garden. Le Nôtre brought in thirty thousand gardeners to execute his vision, favoring geometrically shaped obelisks and spheres rather than the more figurative designs beloved by the Italians. He also installed an elaborate hedge maze, with 39 fountains and 333 statues of animals inside, constructed to entertain Louis's young son. Le Nôtre filled the gardens with yew tree topiaries planted in square wooden boxes that were raised on four feet. Louis XIV was so captivated by them—they perfectly symbolized his mastery over nature—that he threw a Yew Tree Ball in 1745 to celebrate the wedding of his son. The costume ball was attended by fifteen thousand people and Louis XIV showed up dressed as a yew tree topiary. It was here that he met the Marquise de Pompadour, the woman who would become his mistress for the next twenty years.

Highly manicured gardens with sculpted hedge mazes and topiary trees fell out of style in the eighteenth century, in favor of a more naturalistic look. Always trend-conscious, King Louis XVI ripped down his great-grandfather's elaborate maze at Versailles, giving Marie-Antoinette

THE MOVIES MAKE IT LOOK EASY

• • • • • • • • • • • •

In the cult classic film Edward Scissorhands, *Edward wows the neighborhood by creating sculptural masterpieces—dinosaurs, mystical creatures, family portraits—in suburban hedges. While the movie makes the process of creating a topiary seem easy—just a clip and snip and voilà!— the process is much more laborious and lengthy. Patience is a requirement for the designer: a finished plant can take years of planning and work to reach maturity, and must be carefully cultivated and cared for to maintain its shape. A figurative topiary shape usually begins with crafting a wire form, placing it in the ground or pot, and then slowly training the plant—the best of which have small leaves and dense foliage like boxwood—to grow along the cage, encouraged by judicious pruning.*

space to create English-style gardens with flower-filled meadows. In England, however, older topiary gardens remained intact on grand estates like Levens Hall in Cumbria, which still has more than a hundred topiaries visitors can enjoy.

I n the nineteenth century, daughters of nouveau-riche Americans set sail for Europe to gain some cultural polish and be married into

impoverished European nobility, trading cash for titles. Returning to their Newport, Rhode Island, mansions, they modeled their gardens after European estates like Château de Marqueyssac in France's Dordogne Valley. One of the most famous examples of these Gilded Age gardens is Green Animals, overlooking Narragansett Bay, which is named after the more than eighty pieces of topiary found throughout the estate's garden. In 1947, Jacqueline Bouvier (later Kennedy) held her debutante party there. She returned years later with her children, John Jr. and Caroline, to attend the annual Harvest Party held at the mansion, taking photos seated in the topiary armchair.

Jackie's fondness for topiary influenced her redesign of the White House's Rose Garden in 1962 and East Garden in 1963. She hired American philanthropist and horticulturalist Bunny Mellon, who was enamored of miniature topiaries in terra-cotta pots. "I saw them as living, breathing objects," Bunny told the *New York Times* in 2014. While animal-shaped shrubs may not have been appropriate for the White House, at Bunny's suggestion, the East Garden's Eisenhower-era palm trees were ripped out and replaced with square boxwood topiary trees, planted in huge wooden boxes à la Versailles.

Given the time, effort, and attention to detail involved, it might seem like topiary gardens are not for the faint of heart or light of wallet. While perseverance and good hand-eye coordination may be required, it is possible to create a topiary masterpiece on a tight budget. In 1980, Pearl Fryar, an African American can factory engineer and amateur topiary artist, began creating leafy sculptures on the front lawn of his Bishopville, South Carolina, home after rescuing trees and shrubs that local nurseries had thrown away. Today he has three hundred topiaries on his property. If you can't wait the five to ten years that an artist like Pearl devotes to growing each plant— or don't have an expanse of lawn on which to display them—don't despair. Potted versions, live or faux, can be purchased online and on your doorstep by morning. With topiary large enough to stand guard by your front door, or small enough to adorn a desk or dining table, there's one (or more) available for every taste and every budget.

Trestle Table

Eating outdoors at a rustic wooden table—an experience many consider to be the height of informal dining today—actually comes with quite a pedigree. The first trestle tables were used for banquets in the great hall of a castle.

Like our modern picnic table, the trestle table was similar in appearance and construction (or lack of it) to a modern carpenter's sawhorse. The main difference between our picnic table and the trestle table was that the trestle table was more portable. The top was simply an unsecured board placed over wooden trestle legs. It was mobile by necessity. The average castle wouldn't have had a dedicated dining room. Instead, the lord, his family, and guests dined in the largest room, known as the great hall. In addition to functioning as a dining room, it served as a place for receiving guests, so it was essential that the dining table be easy to assemble and disassemble.

In a castle or manor house, you wouldn't have needed a clock to tell you that supper was about to be served. The flurry of servants setting up tables in the great hall would have been signal enough. If there was to be a session of court or an assembly after the meal, the servants would "turn the tables," flipping over the board to the unused side. After the meal or gathering was finished, the table was cleared and the trestles and boards were removed so that the floor could be swept.

Trestle tables were so narrow that diners often sat on only one side, with their backs to the wall. They were usually set up in a horseshoe configuration and covered with a white tablecloth. Not only did this arrange-

THE BOARD

When we talk about the price of meals being included with a room, we refer to "room and board"—the "board" being the top of the trestle table. The words "boardroom" and chairman/woman of the "board" also refer to that tabletop.

ment make food service easier, but it also gave diners a better view of the entertainment; jugglers and musicians often performed during suppertime. And if a fight broke out during the meal (which was not that unusual), you could flip the table over, Wild West style, and use it as a shield.

Where you sat and whom you sat next to was part of an elaborate protocol that would have made even Emily Post nervous. Like the headmaster's table in the Great Hall at Hogwarts, the head of the household and his family sat above the crowd on a dais in the front of the room. Everyone else was seated below the dais. If you were a visitor, you stood by the door and waited for the marshall of the hall to direct you to your place. You'd recognize him by his 27-inch [68.5-cm] staff, which was both a symbol of his authority and handy for breaking up fights between people or dogs.

The beginning of the seventeenth century saw the use of a dedicated room for eating, and the dining table became a fixed piece of furniture. It was a domino effect: Once the table no longer needed to be portable, the top board didn't have to be lightweight. Materials like a thick, heavy wood slab or piece of stone were sturdier and gave more stable support. Even so, the trestle form remained a favorite choice, whether made of more substantial materials for indoor dining or the lighter woods for eating outdoors. Renaissance diners often chose the

portable table for alfresco dinner parties. And in the late nineteenth century, when Monet picnicked at Giverny, it was a trestle table on which the spread of *pâté en croûte* (wild rabbit or duck terrines) and fruit tarts rested.

Today, trestle tables are still a popular choice for dining, indoors and out. Topped with luxe woods or stone, or crafted of sturdy, weather-resistant pine, their simple lines have an enduring appeal and fit in with almost any decor.

A FULL HOUSE

· · · · · · · · · · · ·

From soldiers to servants to extended family, a medieval castle could easily house hundreds of people at any given time. Richard II, for example, had a kitchen staff of three hundred to feed and serve the nearly one thousand people living in his castle each night. Even a duke could expect two hundred people for dinner. Dinnertime would have been a bit like the familiar holiday meal scramble for extra tables and chairs—except you never knew whether someone might show up with an extra fifty guests.

Turkish and Persian Rugs

In 1543, a Turkish carpet was awarded a supporting role in the romantic drama playing out at the royal palace, Château de Fontainebleau. Diane de Poitiers, mistress of King Henri II of France, lay on top of it, entwined in the arms of her lover. In a room above, Henri's wife, Catherine de' Medici, tearfully peered through a peephole in the floor and, according to gossipy court biographer Brantôme, saw "a beautiful, fair woman, fresh and half undressed . . . caressing her lover in a hundred ways, who was doing the same to her." Brantôme reported that Catherine turned away from the scene and complained bitterly that Henri "never used her so well."

At the time, having a carpet on the floor would have been almost as startling as the action on it. Europeans had discovered the deeply colored, elaborately patterned rugs of Turkey and Persia when soldiers and knights brought them home from the Crusades. The rugs immediately became deeply coveted symbols of status, wealth, and power—much too rare and expensive to walk on (never mind to roll around on in wanton abandon).

The Crusaders were not the first conquerors to appreciate these luxurious woven textiles, also called Oriental or Islamic carpets. Persian rugs were a favorite of the Greeks, who snapped them up as spoils of war during their ongoing battles with the Persians. The first mention of their high quality is found around 400 B.C.E. in the writings of the Greek mercenary soldier and historian Xenophon, a student of Socrates, who was impressed by how the plush texture "yielded" underfoot. Centuries later, Venetian merchant Marco Polo was equally bewitched by the rugs he saw in 1270 while traveling through the Anatolia region of the Byzantine Empire, where he discovered "the most beautiful carpets in the world."

Turkey and Persia were part of "the rug belt," where the art of creating hand-woven carpets was practiced in towns and cities and by the nomadic tribes of the region. Persian rugs are woven on a loom using a knotting technique that emperor Darius I, had her own carpet manufacturing facility.

THE WORLD'S MOST LUXURIOUS CARPET

·············

The most extravagant carpet of the ancient world was made in the sixth century for the Persian king Khosrow I. It measured 84 square feet [7.8 sq m], and was woven in a mix of wool and silk with silver and gold threads, lavishly adorned with precious gems. Known as the Winter Carpet, it was designed to evoke the feeling of walking through an elaborate garden of every blossom known to the Persians. The carpet symbolized the king's command over nature. When the Arabs sacked the royal palace in the city of Ctesiphon in 637 C.E., they cut up Khosrow's carpet and gave each soldier a fragment.

In Persian and Turkish culture, carpets could be utilitarian (a floor or wall covering, or prayer rug) or a luxury item. Sometimes they played a symbolic role: Layers of rugs were spread before the Persian emperor as he walked, so that his feet would never touch the ground. (In 1902, the New York Central Railroad channeled the spirit of the Persian emperor's carpeted path when they used red rugs to direct people as they boarded "the world's greatest train": *The 20th Century Limited*. Once on board, passengers received a welcome that was so exclusive that people referred to it as getting the "red carpet treatment.")

In Europe, through the Middle Ages and the Renaissance, prized Oriental carpets were hung on walls or draped over writing and dining tables. (On a dining table, it would be protected by a white tablecloth or removed before the meal.) The only time you would see a carpet on the floor was when the owner (who generally was rich and/or famous) was sitting for a portrait. In her 1563 portrait, for example, Queen Elizabeth I stands on a velvety red Turkish rug that complements her crimson dress—but in reality, the floors of her Great Hall in Greenwich Castle were covered with straw.

creates a carpet with a soft, fleece-like pile. The weaver, often a woman, creates horizontal rows of knots: after each knot, the yarn is cut to create soft pile. The color of the wool used to make the knot is like a single tile in a mosaic. The skills needed to create these magnificent rugs were passed down through hundreds of generations of women weavers. And it's a legacy with quite a pedigree. Around 500 B.C.E., Princess Artystone, daughter of emperor Cyrus the Great and wife of

The growing European demand for Oriental rugs couldn't be satisfied by

the slow trickle of imports and war spoils. To meet the need in the 1600s, textile factories sprung up, particularly in Spain, using the same technology as Princess Artystone's workshop: many looms each operated by a single weaver. They tried to re-create the Middle Eastern rugs, but could not duplicate the saturated colors, designs, or feel of the originals. Despite the subpar quality of the European rugs, still only royalty and the wealthiest merchants could afford them. By the 1700s, carpets were still a luxurious indulgence, but they were more common and slightly less expensive. With an increase in quantity, carpets began to move from the wall to the floor.

It was the Industrial Revolution that paved the way for manufacturers to make carpets, as we know and use them, more widely available. In 1801, Joseph Marie Jacquard exhibited a mechanical loom at the industrial exhibition in Paris. The loom "read" the design of the carpet from wooden punch cards strung together by rope in the same way early computers "read" punch cards. By partially automating the weaving process, the Jacquard loom made it possible to re-create in a few days the complex designs that took a weaver months or sometimes years to complete. Today, the combination of automated looms and synthetic fibers make it possible to buy an 8-by-11-foot [2.4-by-3.4-m] "Oriental" carpet for less than $100. The flood of possibilities for carpet manufacturers led to homes where

rugs and carpets were the rule, rather than the exception. In a world where machine-made carpets are readily available and cheap, automation has only increased our appreciation for—as well as the value of—carpets that are made by hand.

PERSIAN VS. TURKISH CARPETS

. . . .

Given the similarities in construction, motifs, and design, along with the dominance of the color red, Persian and Turkish rugs can be difficult to distinguish. The main differences? First, geography: Though at one time the Persian Empire encompassed two million square miles, most Persian rugs today come from modern-day Iran. Turkish carpets come from, well, Turkey. The second difference? Knots. Persian rugs are made with a single-looping knot, while the Turkish rugs are made of a double knot. The best way to tell the difference if you're not an expert? Check to see whether you can see the pattern on the underside, which is a good indication that it was actually made by hand.

Vase

Whether ordered through a florist or purchased as a grocery store impulse buy, flowers belong in a vase, right? Not so fast. While the Greeks and Romans made exquisitely designed and decorated vases, they weren't intended to hold bouquets. It wasn't that the ancients didn't appreciate flowers and foliage; they did. But those flowers were for wreaths and garlands. Vases were reserved to transport wine, water, and perfume.

By the Middle Ages, flower arrangements had migrated from the wall to the table. They were housed in whatever vessel was handy, which included antique vases. A favorite choice was a lidded vase, where both the cover and the body of the container were pierced; this allowed each flower to stand apart and be appreciated individually. Considering that premium cultivated blooms were often so expensive that it made more financial sense to purchase a painting of them rather than the real thing, this made a certain amount of sense. (It also explains why there are so many floral still lifes gracing museum walls.)

It wasn't only the flowers that were pricey. These days, when porcelain is so common that even our toilets are made from it, it's hard to fathom a time when it was once so rare that it seemed almost magical. Porcelain had been invented in China thousands

VASE LAMPS

. . . .

In prehistoric China, gourds were prized as vessels for holding water. Early potters modeled their ceramic vases on the organic shape, with tapered necks and one or two bulbous rounds. When porcelain was invented, the same shape was replicated in this new lustrous material.

In the 1700s, gourd vases were collected, prized, and displayed throughout Europe. When Joseph Swan developed the incandescent light bulb in 1878, the invention gave the vessels new life. Like most wealthy British aristocrats, Sir William Armstrong had a stash of porcelain gourd vases. He married the new light source to one of them, and used it as a table lamp for his desk. It was the world's first electric lamp.

of years earlier, but was completely unknown in Europe until the Renaissance, when Europe's love affair with it began. And not any generic Chinese porcelain would do; it was vases made during the time of the Ming dynasty that captured the hearts and wallets of Europe. Recognized by its crisp blue artwork on a bright white or milky background, Ming porcelain was thinner and more translucent than anything else on the market.

Although the dynasty lasted from 1368 to 1644, vases in the Ming style continued to be made and exported. Europe's obsession reached its peak in the early eighteenth century. Augustus the Strong, the ruler of Dresden, bought 151 of them from the ruler of Berlin and paid for them not with money, but with 600 of his soldiers.

As eighteenth-century collectors knew, whether filled with flowers or left empty, a vase can add a little pizazz to a room. Authentic Ming vases are very rare and extremely valuable. In 2012, Sotheby's sold one for $1.3 million at auction. But there's still hope for those who get bitten by the blue and white bug. The craft is being revitalized by young Chinese artisans in Jingdezhen, China, where the vases were first produced seven hundred years ago.

Tastes shifted in the 1750s, when excavations at Herculaneum and Pompeii provided new inspiration for European artists and designers. The classic vase shapes of ancient Greece and Rome became all the rage. Manufacturers rushed to meet the demand with copies, but if you could afford it, there was nothing quite like the real thing.

Sir William Hamilton, British ambassador to the Kingdom of Naples from 1764 to 1800, had a nose for both the genuine article and those with deep enough pockets to pay handsomely for them. During the time of his appointment, he managed to send (quite literally) boatloads of antique vessels back to England. One of those was a small, not quite 10-inch- [25-cm-] tall vase of deep and translucent cobalt blue with seven figures carved out of opaque white glass overlay. The cameo technique—etching and carving through fused layers of differently colored glass to produce designs—was the height of innovation in Rome when it was made. It was equally captivating to the fashionable set in eighteenth-century London.

Hamilton had a target in mind: the Duchess of Portland. She was known to be utterly obsessed with antique vases and just happened to be the richest woman in Britain. (She's also the great-great-great-great grandmother of Queen Elizabeth II.) One of her friends said that she was "a simple woman, but perfectly sober and intoxicated only by empty vases." She snapped up the prize for £4,000 (about £475,000, or $610,000, today).

Like the rest of his countrymen, the great British potter Josiah Wedgwood was intrigued by what became known as the Portland Vase. He had already established a profitable business producing containers that echoed both the shape and the color of antique originals. Wedgwood spent four years and thousands of trials working to create an exact replica of the duchess's vase. In the process, he created jasperware, a fine-grained stoneware that would be his greatest technical innovation. Wedgwood said that he wanted to be "Vase Maker General to the Universe," and he achieved just

that. He put his vase on display in London and sold tickets for view. It created such a frenzy that people had to be turned away. Wedgwood was propelled to celebrity status and made a fortune in the process.

Today the vase often takes second place to the flowers in them. Inexpensive glass in a variety of shapes, sizes, and colors has replaced porcelain as the material of choice. Rather than a collector's item, the ubiquitous florist's vase is as disposable as a two-week-old bouquet. But with a little effort, you can find craftspeople creating vases of blown glass, hand-thrown pottery, and even lacquered paper that are as unique and beautiful as the flowers that they're meant to hold.

Wallpaper

Paleolithic Age paintings in the caves of Lascaux. Murals in Egypt. Frescos of Pompeii. Intricate tapestries that decorated the castles of the Middle Ages and the palaces of the Renaissance. Let's face it: The urge to decorate walls and personalize a space spans the course of human civilization.

> **"Whatever you have in your rooms, think first of the walls, for they are that which makes your House and Home. . ."**
>
> —WILLIAM MORRIS

Portability was a central design component throughout the Middle Ages and the Renaissance. Wall decoration (and furniture) commonly moved from room to room and from castle to castle as great households moved between vast estates. Removable wall furnishings made decorating relatively easy—useful when you might not be in one place too long, or had to leave quickly.

For centuries, tapestries were the gold standard of wall decoration. Both ornamental and practical, they beautified and insulated the cold gray walls of drafty castles. By the time of the Renaissance, all the great artists, including Michelangelo, Raphael, and Da Vinci, designed tapestries. The only downside? They were not only hard on the wallet, but also time-consuming—think years—to create.

In 1481, Louis XI came up with an ingenious solution: He commissioned court painter Jean Bourdichon to paint fifty paper scrolls with the first lines of Psalm 89 in Latin. The rolls, which adorned his bedroom, were hung like window roller shades, rather than applied with paste or glue. Louis commissioned angel holders, like a modern curtain rod, so that the papers could easily be hung up and taken down.

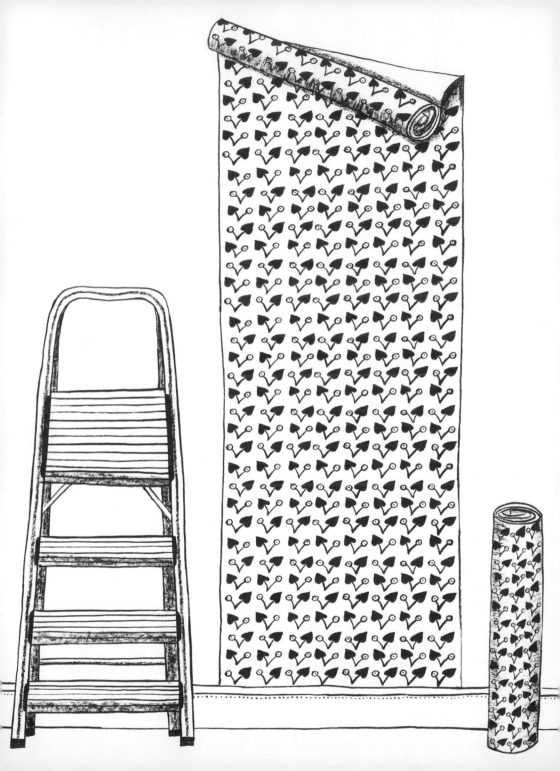

In the sixteenth century, when tea merchants—always on the lookout for new products to sell—began bringing rolls of decorative rice paper back from China with their tea cargo, Europe took notice. The Chinese had been hanging rice paper painted with genealogical charts, deities, and landscapes on their walls for thousands of years before the concept took hold in the West. And while paper might not have had the same warmth of a Da Vinci tapestry or the prestige of Louis XI's meticulously hand-painted calligraphy, it did come with a smaller price tag—and the advantage of immediate gratification.

Looking to fill the gap for those without a king-size decorating budget, seventeenth-century French craftsmen produced *dominos*, or single sheets of decorated papers about 14 inches [35.5 cm] wide by 20 inches [50 cm] long. They were printed in black with a single carved block and painted by hand, using a stencil, for a little additional color. More affordable and extremely popular as wall decoration, the papers could be joined together and pasted on a wall to make a larger pattern; they were also used individually to decorate everything from books to boxes.

Hand printing and hand painting paper was both expensive and time-consuming, keeping wallpaper out of the reach of all but the wealthiest consumers. In the eighteenth century, the DIY movement took hold, and well-to-do British women embraced "print rooms." In these dedicated spaces, the walls served as large canvases for elaborate collages, composed of favorite prints that were pasted directly to the wall. They finished the look with printed frames, borders, and decorative motifs like ribbons and swags to complement and unify the design, which was sealed with a coat of varnish. It was a favorite way to spend a rainy afternoon with friends: an eighteenth-century scrapbooking party.

It wasn't until the Industrial Revolution that wallpaper could be produced cheaply and in enough quantity to make it affordable for nearly every segment of the population. But convenience can come with a price, and early mass-produced wallpaper came with a hefty one: By the late nineteenth century, 80 percent of English wall coverings contained arsenic-based greens. (Arsenic creates a vibrant and intense shade of green. And while it was a known poison, the prevailing view was that it could only cause harm if it was ingested, which was not the case.) People were being slowly poisoned in their own homes, which may explain why, in many cases, a "change of air" was often a successful treatment for the chronically ill. Even the wealthiest and most powerful individuals weren't immune. On his deathbed, Oscar Wilde said, "This wallpaper and I are fighting a duel to the death. Either it goes or I do." Although Wilde, who hated wallpaper, was referring to the soul-crushing ugliness of his Left Bank hotel room, much of the wallpaper was, at the time, indeed lethal.

A VELVET TOUCH

. . . .

Flocked wallpapers, often ornately patterned with a textured, velvety finish, got a bit of a bad rap after their overuse in the 1970s—but they have come back with a vengeance.

Flock is a powdered wool that was a by-product of the woolen mill industry. It was applied to papers starting around 1600 as a less expensive alternative to the cut velvet that was en vogue. To create flocked paper, a design was stenciled over a painted background color with slow-drying adhesive; the flock was scattered on top to produce a velvety pile.

The craze for textured paper took off in 1715, and everyone who was anyone installed it. Even Madame de Pompadour, Louis XV's trendsetting mistress, had flocked wallpapers installed in her apartment at Versailles. The papers were fashionable until the mid-nineteenth century, when the Victorians came to prefer washable, "sanitary" wallpaper over the potentially germ-trapping and difficult-to-clean flocked variety.

Napoleon experienced this firsthand. Three weeks before his death at age fifty-one, he wrote from exile on the island of St. Helena, "I die before my time, murdered by the English oligarchy and its assassin." He was right about dying before his time, but the culprit wasn't the English oligarchy. Modern tests of the brilliant green wallpaper in his bedroom revealed that it was saturated with arsenic—which, in the hot, damp climate of St. Helena, would have given off significant toxic fumes.

The fashion for papered rooms ebbs and flows. In recent years, wallpaper has experienced a resurgence. But don't get too comfortable. History proves that just as the glue has dried, wallpaper is declared "out" and you're scraping it off again.

Windsor Chair

When you look at a spindle-back Windsor chair, it might conjure up visions of a New England bed-and-breakfast with a white picket fence, blueberry pancakes for breakfast, and apple picking on the afternoon agenda, the sort of place that's "as American as apple pie." You'd be right. In fact, it would be hard to find another piece of furniture with stronger connections to the founding fathers of the United States. George Washington lined the porch of his Mount Vernon home with twenty-seven bow-backed Windsor chairs. John Adams had Windsor chairs at his farm in Quincy, Massachusetts, and Thomas Jefferson sat in a custom-made revolving version (the first swivel chair) as he drafted the Declaration of Independence. And on July 4, 1776, when Congress voted on independence for the colonies in the Assembly Room of the Pennsylvania State House, the fifty-six delegates were seated in Windsor chairs. And perhaps it was the Windsor chair he sat in that inspired Henry Wadsworth Longfellow to write his famous poem, "Paul Revere's Ride," eighty-five years after the Declaration signing.

There's more than a little irony in America's patriotic love for the Windsor chair: The design and name of the object actually came from across the pond. Legend has it that King George III, who ruled Great Britain from 1760 to 1820, was caught in a sudden downpour while hunting in his five-thousand-acre Windsor Great Park. Taking shelter in a peasant's cottage, he was seated in a chair with a curved spindle back and carved-out saddle seat, and found it extremely comfortable. Whether the story is apocryphal or not, the chair was most certainly used in the Windsor Castle garden, from which it got its name. With the royal seal of approval, the Windsor soon became the most popular garden chair in the country. There was even a version of the seat built on a platform on wheels that could be pushed around the garden by a servant for the frail, the lazy, or those who simply didn't want to put on their shoes (or get them dirty) for a garden stroll. This prototype became one of the earlier European examples of a wheelchair.

By the late 1750s, the English Windsor chair had become ubiquitous indoors as well as outdoors, and was used everywhere from inns and taverns to libraries and meetinghouses. The main design difference between the English and American versions is the use of a splat (a middle piece in the back of the chair) in British chairs; Americans preferred the low-back Windsor. At a time when the American and British could agree on little else, they were unified on the appeal of this beloved domestic object.

By the time of the American Revolution, furniture making was big business in the colonies. Furnishings were much too expensive for most people to ship, so unless a person had deep pockets, such objects were locally made. Colonial carpenters pored over stylebooks from Europe and crafted their own versions using local wood. Philadelphia wood crafters were the first to experiment with the Windsor format, and it became an instant hit.

One of the major selling points of the chair was its portability: It was lightweight and easy to carry from room to room. Both English and American Windsors were usually made of three different woods for structural and design reasons. The legs and stretchers (the pieces of wood that stretch between the legs for added support) were a hardwood like maple, walnut, or cherry, which could be lathe-turned to create sharp edges. The seats were a softwood like pine or tulipwood that was easier to carve into a saddle shape. The characteristic spindles, which gave the back that comfortable curve, were made of hickory, a wood that can bend without breaking. (In fact, it's the shape of the back rail that identifies the variations on the classic Windsor design: hoop back, fan back, bow back, low back, comb back, or brace back.) The whole thing was painted to unify the different wood tones, although eighteenth-century DIY enthusiasts could purchase unpainted chairs and give them a custom color at home.

The Windsor chair wins popularity contests—not only with decorating enthusiasts, but also with some of the biggest names in twentieth-century design. In 1946, furniture designer George Nakashima created his modernist homage to the traditional Windsor—the Straight Chair—in his New Hope, Pennsylvania, workshop, not far from where the original American Windsors were first crafted. Other designers still aspired to create something as lasting and durable. In the 1970s, American designer Charles Eames, who created the iconic wood and leather Eames chair, told a reporter how much he admired the form: "I have always hoped my chairs would be regarded as the Windsors of the twentieth century." With versions of the classic Windsor chair still sold in nearly every furniture store and gracing the pages of almost every design magazine, it turns out it's the Windsor that is the Windsor of the twentieth century.

Wineglass

Today, there are almost as many different types of wineglasses as there were forks on the Victorian table. It's no longer a simple question of red, white, or sparkling. There's a glass made for every varietal, designed to enhance every aspect of taste. Some are made to target where the wine lands on your tongue; some have a larger bowl to allow a bouquet to fully develop; still others help aeration with a rippled shape for a better swirl.

Although glass was invented more than 3,500 years ago (probably in Egypt or Mesopotamia), the birth of the wineglass as we know it dates to 50 B.C.E. That was when the single greatest leap forward in glass manufacturing occurred: The blowpipe was invented in Syria (then part of the Roman Empire). According to legend, a manufacturer was attempting to clear molten glass from the end of a clogged hollow pipe. When he blew into it, he created a bubble. From the bubble, a skilled glassmaker could quickly form the molten substance into any number of shapes. This was a huge improvement over the Egyptian method, in which the glass was spun around a core (usually made of dung and clay). The core then had to be laboriously picked out once the glass had hardened.

The blowpipe technique enabled a variety of products to be produced quickly and in larger quantities. Rather than transport the fragile items, it was the glassmakers who were exported to the farthest reaches of the empire. There was so much glass available, and it was so cheap, that if a wineglass chipped, a Roman housewife would simply throw it away and buy a new one.

IT DON'T MEAN A THING IF IT AIN'T GOT THAT PING

. . . .

If you're looking to discern Venetian glass from lead crystal, just tap it with your fingernail. A loud ping is the tell-tale sign of crystal made from barium or zinc. Potassium-based Venetian glass makes a much softer sound.

"Considering the short life [of glass], due to its fragility, one cannot and must not give it too much love, and one must use it and understand it as an example of the life of man and of the things of this world which, though beautiful, are transitory and frail."

—*VANNOCCIO BIRINGUCCIO,*
DE LA PIROTECHNIA, 1540, FROM THE
SECTION ON GLASSMAKING

The glass added to the appreciation of that favorite Roman beverage: wine. The earliest glass drinking vessels, called tumblers, were made with rounded or pointed bases. They were intended to be held, not placed on the table. When full, they were sta-ble because the weight of the liquid prevented the vessel from tipping over—but empty, they toppled. To keep the beverage cool, the vessels were planted upright in the ground or a river and then delivered to the table as needed.

But during the Middle Ages, much glassmaking knowledge, like so much else, was lost. Glassware became so rare that wine-glasses were made with extra-large bowls for sharing.

Although glassmaking declined in Europe, Roman traditions were retained throughout the Middle East. When the city of Constantinople was sacked by the Fourth Crusade in 1204, many artisans fled to Venice, which has been the glassmaking center of the Western world ever since.

The city became a hub of creative innovation. In the fourteenth century, Venetian glassmakers invented cris-tallo. Named for its resemblance to cut quartz, the relatively clear glass was made with soda ash imported from Spain. The technique was one that had been used by the Romans, but was lost during the intervening centuries. Cris-tallo was thin and pliable, and orna-mentation was limited to the form of the vessel, rather than applied surface decorations. Venetian glass was (and still is) characterized by goblets shaped with elaborate stems in the shapes of wings, dragons, or mythical creatures. It was the most sought-after glass in Europe—and not just because people loved beautiful objects. In the poison-fearing medieval world, it was believed that cristallo would spontaneously crack and shatter if a poisonous liquid was poured into it.

Possessing fine glassware was a sign of aristocratic status. Venetian wine was usually drunk from a wineglass called a *tazza*. It was precariously shallow to better aerate the wine, but almost nearly impossible to drink from splash-free. (The better you were at avoiding spills, the more sophisticated you appeared.)

It would take another hundred years, but finally the British surged ahead of continental Europe when George Ravenscroft invented lead crystal. Adding lead oxide both improved the clarity of the glass and made it easier to melt. This new material was a formi-

dable rival to the Venetian cristallo. Not only was it cheaper, but it was also easier to facet. Soon, light-refracting, cut-crystal glasses were a must on every Victorian table. But while the sparkling glassware may have delighted hostesses, the lead in the crystal was slowly poisoning imbibers. In fact, symptoms of gout prevalent throughout the nineteenth century were the result of the lead in the crystal decanters and glasses that graced upper-class tables. Thankfully, by the 1990s most crystal was made with barium or zinc instead of lead, in order to prevent illness.

Like everything else in modern life, glassware choices abound. If you're suffering decision fatigue, just think of the joke: What's the best glass for wine? The one you're holding.

Wreath and Garland

In the fifth century B.C.E., the last emperor of Persia, Darius III, employed forty-six wreath makers in his palace at Persepolis, now in modern-day Iran. (There were also seventy people in his palace whose sole responsibility was to pour wine. Clearly, Darius believed in having a good time.) When Alexander the Great conquered the Persian Empire, he spared the lives of the palace servants, who were forcibly added to his household. The expert floral decorators immediately began making wreaths and garlands for their new king's military campaign, which already had a reputation as a roving party (fighting by day, revelry by night). Guests arriving at one of Alexander's raucous flower-bedecked fetes would be presented at the door with a circle woven of ivy and parsley to wear on their head during the festivities, similar to a party hat. As a bonus, the scent of some leaves and flowers used in the garlands, particularly rose and myrtle, was thought to prevent drunkenness. (Not that it worked well for Alexander, whose drunken brawls were as legendary as his wartime conquests.)

Alexander's army brought the Persian prisoners back to Greece. These captives spread the art of braiding flowers and leaves, and soon it became an important part of Greek culture. At parties, the Greek sculptures that fill our museums today were festooned with garlands and crowned with wreaths. Leafy diadems were also bestowed on beloved athletes to recognize their achievements. In fact, it's thanks to those athletes that the wreath transitioned from headgear to the wall. Proud athletes would hang their hard-won laurel circlet on their front doors to oh-so-casually let the community know about their achievements. A similar tradition was used to announce the honorific birth of a male child in Athens: A wreath made of olive branches was hung on the doors of the porticos, the precursor to the front porch. If the baby was a girl, the door was decorated with a ribbon of wool to represent the household responsibilities to which she would devote herself.

For a Roman family, social standing derived from the public service of their men. A wreath carved above the door was a signal that a male member of the household had saved another Roman citizen in battle. The decoration is thought to have morphed from an impermanent object into a permanent fixture when the Senate honored the first Roman emperor, Augustus, with a stone laurel and oak leaf wreath carved over his front door. It was created in recognition of the emperor's triumph over Marc Antony and Cleopatra at the Battle of Actium in 31 B.C.E.

During the Middle Ages, wreaths became a symbol of love. Ladies would give headbands of roses to their paramours. When artists painted young lovers, they were pictured wearing wreaths, symbolizing their shared passion. We can still see remnants of this tradition today, as many brides walk down the aisle wearing a flower crown.

The language of leaves and flowers is a timeless and universal one. While Western cultures made use of both wreaths and garlands, cords of entwined blossoms were, and are, an essential part of Indian culture. Women wear ropes of jasmine in their hair, and couples exchange garlands called *varmala* three times at their weddings. Strings of colorful and fragrant flowers decorate doorframes and statues of Hindu deities. Each god

BLOSSOMS FOR THE BLUSHING BRIDE

• • • • • • • • • • • •

When Queen Victoria wed Prince Albert in 1840, she wore an orange blossom wreath in her hair and set off a floral craze. Orange blossoms became so closely associated with weddings that "to gather orange blossoms" meant "to look for a wife."

or goddess has his or her own leaf or flower: hibiscus leaves for Laitha, the flower *jaba* for Kali, and *tulasi* (holy basil) leaves for Vishnu.

The eighteenth-century neoclassical fascination with all things Greek and Roman resulted in a full-on obsession with wreaths and garlands. Chains of real and artificial flowers were draped over everything from pictures and statues to door and window frames, and became an essential component of party decor. In another nod to classical Roman fashion, painted or carved versions also decorated doorways, walls, and windows. When Queen Charlotte of England held a ball to celebrate the anniversary of King George III's accession to the throne in 1793, she put her favorite daughter, Princess Elizabeth, in charge of the decorations. The princess enlisted the assistance of her friends and other female members of the household to make an artificial flower garland that was

1,000 yards [914 m] long. She then hired an architect who spent a week helping her design a decorating scheme centered around their creation.

These days, our athletes and heroes wear medals, not laurel leaves. But wreaths still play a role in welcoming guests to our home. They celebrate the seasons, made of colorful spring flowers, autumn-hued leaves, or elegant bare twigs. There are circles of pastel eggs for Easter, black bats for Halloween, or turkeys for Thanksgiving. And of course, the Christmas evergreen wreath takes us back to the Romans, who would give green boughs shaped into a circle on New Year's Day as a symbol of well wishes for the coming year. How fitting for an eternal symbol from the eternal city!

Acknowledgments

As I sit surrounded by two hundred borrowed books from both the University of California, Davis Library and the Sacramento Public Library, I am indebted to the existence of libraries and their lenient loan policies. In particular, Eric Webb from Sacramento Public Library and Robin Gustafson at UC Davis, for adroitly helping me avoid late fees. I'm in great debt to the digital collection of the Victoria & Albert Museum, in particular the descriptions for jewelry boxes and punch bowls that guided my research and understanding of those objects.

The bibliography is a road map of my journey through the secondary source material that I relied on to educate me about a subject. I returned frequently to the works of Mandy Aftel and Joan DeJean, whose style and mastery of their respective subjects were inspirational. Witold Rybczynski's *Home: A Short History of an Idea* started me down the path of decorative arts history nearly ten years ago. I shall remain ever grateful to the instructors in the History of Design and Decorative Arts program at Parsons/Cooper-Hewitt—particularly Donald Albrecht, Laura Auricchio, David Brody, Cheryl Buckley, Sarah Lawrence, and Ethan Robey—for grounding me in the subject.

I became a student in Barry Rice's copyediting class when I was a college sophomore and subsequently took every class he taught. My interest in design dovetailed with his own, and later, when he became a designer in New York, he gamely took me along on his decorating jobs. He has been a constant, unwavering supporter and cheerleader for me both personally and professionally and is one of my most treasured friends.

I'm grateful to my colleagues at UC Davis for supporting me while I worked on this project: Peter Brantley, Kimmy Hescock, Quinn Hart, Neil Weingarten, Dale Snapp, Jessica Nausbaum, Beth Callahan, and MacKenzie Smith.

I am forever indebted to Grace Bonney for giving me my first platform to write about design history. And thank you to Amanda Sims for giving me a space to continue. Thank you to Jaime Derringer for allowing me to be part of the Design Milk team. And to Irma Zandl for her wise mentorship and encouragement.

ACKNOWLEDGMENTS

To the team at Chronicle Books: Thank you to Rachel Hiles for believing in this project and helping to shape it. Thank you to illustrator Alice Pattullo for helping bring these objects to life. And thank you to Rachel Harrell for her design efforts and Karen Levy for copyediting.

Writing is only half of making a book. Magnolia Molcan, Meghan Legg, Madeline Moe, Cynthia Shannon, Joyce Lin, and everyone at Chronicle have worked so hard to put this book into the hands of those who love design.

Thanks to Liana Allday for her early editorial support and constant positivity. To Allison Task, whose encouragement and clear thinking guided me during personal transitions while ensuring that I kept focus on professional ones.

And to my beloved agent, Judy Liden, for her warmth, encouragement, and unwavering belief in me. There most certainly would not be a book without you. And there are not enough "thank you" synonyms in the thesaurus to express my gratitude.

To my dear friend and inspiration, Jessica Oreck: Our weekly accountability emails both helped keep me on track and provided some welcome distraction.

Every person deserves a Rebecca Federman. She has sat with me in silence when life sometimes felt like it got the upper hand and rejoiced with me when I succeeded. Her capacity for listening knows no bounds. I know. I have tested it.

Thanks to my siblings: sisters Dorie and Shelley, their husbands, Kelvin and Wyatt, and brother Matthew. You are all my greatest champions. And thank you to their children, Ethan, Harper, Emma, Hadley, and Cooper, for being the most engaging and charming distractions one could imagine. I can't wait to see what you all become.

And to my mother- and father-in-law, Dot and Ken Fujiwara, who have always treated me as a daughter, without hyphens. Thank you for your continued love and support and all you do to make Mark's and my life easier.

Thank you to my parents, Robert and Susan Azzarito, who raised me in a home filled with books, good design, and a belief in expansiveness of the world's possibilities, and who instilled in me a resilience that came in handy during the six years of working on this project.

To my five-wek-old newborn, Stella Dot, who naps in my arms as I finish this book: Thank you for grounding me in the present and demonstrating the joys of curiousity and learning.

This book is dedicated to my husband, Mark Fujiwara. My world is a better place since you came along. Thank you for bringing your grace, good humor, energy, and enthusiasm to every moment of our life together.

Selected Bibliography

Bathtub

Dalby, Andrew. *Empire of Pleasure: Luxury and Indulgence in the Roman World*. London: Routledge, 2000.

de Bonneville, Francoise. *The Book of the Bath*. New York: Rizzoli, 1998.

Grilli, Peter. *Furo: The Japanese Bath*. Tokyo: Kodansha International, 1985.

von Furstenberg, Diane. *The Bath*. New York: Random House, 1993.

Wright, Lawrence. *Clean and Decent: The Fascinating History of the Bathroom and the Water Closet*. New York: Viking Press, 1960.

Billiard Table

Baird, Sarah. "The Life and Death of the American Pool Hall." *Punch*, January 23, 2015. Accessed July 11, 2017. http://punchdrink .com/articles/the-life- and-death-of-the -american-pool-hall.

Levron, Jacques. *Daily Life in Versailles in the Seventeenth and Eighteenth Centuries*. New York: The Macmillan Company, 1968.

Stein, Victor, and Paul Rubinol. *The Billiard Encyclopedia: An Illustrated History of the Sport*. Minneapolis, MN: Blue Book Publications, 1996.

Bookshelf

Mari, Francesca. "Shelf Conscious." *Paris Review*, December 27, 2012. https://www.theparis review.org/blog/2012 /12/27/shelf-conscious.

Petroski, Henry. *The Book on the Bookshelf*. New York: Vintage Books, 2000.

Picon, Guillaume. *Versailles: A Private Invitation*. Paris: Flammarion, 2017.

Tye, Larry. *The Father of Spin: Edward Bernays and the Birth of Public Relations*. New York: Crown Publishers, 1998.

Candle

Bremer-David, Charissa, ed. *Paris: Life and Luxury in the Eighteenth Century*. Los Angeles: J. Paul Getty Trust, 2011.

Dillon, Maureen. *Artificial Sunshine: A Social History of Domestic Lighting*. London: The National Trust, 2002.

Neimeyer, Charles Patrick. *The Revolutionary War*. Westport, CT: Greenwood Press, 2007.

Snodgrass, Mary Ellen. *Encyclopedia of Kitchen History*. New York: Fitzroy Dearborn, 2004.

Canopy Bed

Bard Graduate Center. *History of Design: Decorative Arts and Material Culture, 1400–2000*. New York: Bard Graduate Center, 2013.

Carlano, Anne, and Bobbie Sumberg. *Sleeping Around: The Bed from Antiquity to Now.* Seattle, WA: University of Washington Press, 2006.

Durant, David N. *Where Queen Elizabeth Slept and What the Butler Saw: Historical Terms from the Sixteenth Century to the Present.* New York: St. Martin's Griffin, 1998.

Gentle, Nicola. "A Study of Late Seventeenth-Century State Bed From Melville House." *Furniture History* 37 (2001): 1–16.

Sarti, Raffaella. *Europe at Home: Family and Material Culture, 1500–1800.* New Haven, CT: Yale University Press, 2004.

Thornton, Peter. *Seventeenth-Century Interior Decoration in England, France and Holland.* New Haven, CT: Yale University Press, 1990.

Wright, Lawrence. *Warm and Snug: The History of the Bed.* Stroud, UK: Sutton, 2004.

Chaise Longue

de Dampierre, Florence. *Chairs: A History.* New York: Harry N. Abrams, 2006.

DeJean, Joan. *The Age of Comfort: When Paris Discovered Casual and the Modern Home Began.* New York: Bloomsbury Press, 2013.

Johnson, Peter. *The Phillips Guide to Chairs.* London: Premier, 1993.

Champagne Coupe

Dunne, Patrick. *The Epicurean Collector: Exploring the World of Culinary Antiques.* Boston: Little, Brown, 2002.

von Drachenfels, Suzanne. *The Art of the Table: A Complete Guide to Table Setting, Table Manners, and Tableware.* New York: Simon & Schuster, 2008.

Chess Set

Brown, Nancy Marie. *Ivory Vikings: The Mystery of the Most Famous Chessmen in the World and the Woman Who Made Them.* Prince Frederick, MD: Recorded Books, 2015.

Dean, George, with Maxine Brady. *Chess Masterpieces: One Thousand Years of Extraordinary Chess Sets.* New York: Abrams Books, 2010.

Shenk, David. *The Immortal Game: A History of Chess.* New York: Doubleday, 2006.

Yalom, Marilyn. *The Birth of the Chess Queen: How Her Majesty Transformed the Game.* New York: HarperCollins, 2004.

Chiavari Chair

de Dampierre, Florence. *Chairs: A History.* New York: Harry N. Abrams, 2006.

Chopsticks

Visser, Margaret. *The Rituals of Dinner: The Origins, Evolution, Eccentricities, and Meaning of Table Manners.* New York: Penguin Books, 1992.

Wang, Edward Q. *Chopsticks: A Culture and Culinary History.* Cambridge, UK: Cambridge University Press, 2015.

Wilson, Bee, and Annabel Lee. *Consider the Fork: A History of How We Cook and Eat.* New York: Basic Books, 2013.

Clock

Bremer-David, Charissa, ed. *Paris: Life and Luxury in the Eighteenth Century.* Los Angeles: J. Paul Getty Museum, 2011.

Chevallier, Bernard, and Marc Walter. *Empire Splendor: French Taste in the Age of Napoleon.* New York: The Vendome Press, 2008.

Ekirch, A. Roger. *At Day's Close: Night in Times Past.* New York: Norton, 2006.

Goodman, Ruth. *How to Be a Victorian: A Dawn-to-Dusk Guide to Victorian Life.* New York: Liveright Publishing, 2015.

James, Peter, and Nick Thorpe. *Ancient Inventions.* New York: Ballantine Books, 1995.

Martyn, Trea. *Elizabeth in the Garden: A Story of Love, Rivalry and Spectacular Design.* London: Faber, 2009.

Moore, June, and Doris Moore. *The Pleasure of Your Company.* London: Rich & Cowan, Ltd., 1936.

Thorndike, Joseph Jacobs. *The Magnificent Builders and Their Dream Houses.* New York: American Heritage Publishing Co., 1978.

Vincent, Clare, J. H. Leopold, and Elizabeth Sullivan. *European Clocks and Watches in the Metropolitan Museum of Art.* New Haven, CT: Yale University Press, 2015.

Cocktail Shaker

Grimes, William. *Straight Up or on the Rocks: The Story of the American Cocktail.* New York: North Point Press, 2001.

Lanza, Joseph. *The Cocktail: The Influence of Spirits on the American Psyche.* New York: St. Martin's Press, 1995.

Crystal Chandelier

Cooke, Lawrence S. *Lighting in America: From Colonial Rushlights to Victorian Chandeliers.* Pittstown, NJ: Main Street Press, 1984.

Fioratti, Helen Costantino. *Illuminating Their World: Three Hundred Years of Light.* New York: L'Antiquaire and the Connoisseur, Inc., 2007.

McCaffety, Kerri. *The Chandelier Through the Centuries: A History of Great European Styles.* New Orleans, LA: Vissi d'Arte Books, 2006.

Curule Chair

de Dampierre, Florence. *Chairs: A History.* New York: Harry N. Abrams, 2006.

Miller, Judith. *Furniture: World Styles from Classical to Contemporary.* London: DK, 2011.

Rybczynski, Witold. *Now I Sit Me Down: From Klismos to Plastic Chair: A Natural History.* New York: Farrar, Straus and Giroux, 2016.

Deck Chair

Rybczynski, Witold. *Now I Sit Me Down: From Klismos to Plastic Chair: A Natural History.* New York: Farrar, Straus and Giroux, 2016.

Desk

Goodman, Dena, and Kathryn Norberg. *Furnishing the Eighteenth Century: What Furniture Can Tell Us about the European and American Past.* New York: Routledge, 2011.

Dollhouse

Broomhall, Susan, Jennifer Spinks, and Allyson M. Poska. *Early Modern Women in the Low Countries: Feminizing Sources and Interpretations of the Past.* Farnham, UK: Taylor and Francis, 2016.

Eaton, Faith. *Classic Dolls' Houses.* London: Phoenix Illustrated, 1997.

Lambton, Lucinda. *Queen's Dolls' House.* London: Royal Collection Trust, 2011.

Pasierbska, Halina. *Dollhouses from the V&A Museum of Childhood.* London: V & A Publishing, 2008.

von Wilckens, L., and Helga Schmidt-Glassner. *The Dolls' House: An Illustrated History.* London: Bell & Hyman, 1980.

Door, Knocker, and Knob

Derry, Nancy E. *Architectural Hardware: Ideas, Inspiration and Practical Advice for Adding Handles, Hinges, Knobs and Pulls to Your Home.* Gloucester, MA: Quarry Books, 2006.

Jütte, Daniel. *The Strait Gate: Thresholds and Power in Western History.* New Haven, CT: Yale University Press, 2015.

Duvet

Worsley, Lucy. *If Walls Could Talk: An Intimate History of the Home.* New York: Walker and Co., 2012.

Wright, Lawrence. *Warm & Snug: The History of the Bed.* Stroud, UK: Sutton, 2004.

Fireplace

Gowlett, J. A. J. "The Discovery of Fire by Humans: A Long and Convoluted Process." *Philosophical Transactions of the Royal Society B: Biological Sciences* 371, no. 1696 (May 2016): 1697-1700.

Lind, Carla. *Frank Lloyd Wright's Fireplaces.* San Francisco: Pomegranate, 1995.

Sarti, Raffaella. *Europe at Home: Family and Material Culture, 1500–1800.* New Haven, CT: Yale University Press, 2004.

Stearns, Peter N. *American Behavioral History: An Introduction.* New York: New York University Press, 2005.

Thornton, Peter. *Authentic Decor: The Domestic Interior, 1620–1920.* London: Weidenfeld & Nicolson, 1984.

Wheelis, Allen. *The Way We Are.* New York: W.W. Norton, 2006.

Worsley, Lucy. *If Walls Could Talk: An Intimate History of the Home.* New York: Walker and Co., 2012.

Flokati Rug

Sebastian, Don. *The Complete Handbook of Flokati and Carpet Making.* Athens: Nick Kokkinos, 1978.

Floral Centerpiece

Belden, Louise Conway. *The Festive Tradition: Table Decoration and Desserts in America, 1650–1900.* New York: W.W. Norton, 1983.

Berrall, Julia. *A History of Flower Arrangement.* London: Thames and Hudson, 1953.

Blacker, Mary Rose. *Flora Domestica: A History of British Flower Arranging, 1500–1930.* New York: Harry N. Abrams, 2000.

Visser, Margaret. *The Rituals of Dinner: The Origins, Evolution, Eccentricities, and Meaning of Table Manners.* New York: Penguin Books, 1992.

Fork

Heugel, Inès. *Laying the Elegant Table: China, Faience, Porcelain, Majolica, Glassware, Flatware, Tureens, Platters, Trays, Centerpieces, Tea Sets.* New York: Rizzoli, 2006.

Lupton, Ellen, et al. *Feeding Desire: Design and the Tools of the Table, 1500–2005.* New York: Assouline, 2006.

von Drachenfels, Suzanne. *The Art of the Table: A Complete Guide to Table Setting, Table Manners, and Tableware.* New York: Simon & Schuster, 2008.

Front Porch

Donlon, Jocelyn Hazelwood. *Swinging in Place: Porch Life in Southern Culture.* Chapel Hill, NC: University of North Carolina Press, 2001.

Goldstein, B. Colleen. *The Evolution and Significance of the Front Porch in American Culture.* Master's dissertation, University of Georgia, 1998.

Kaye, Myrna. *There's a Bed in the Piano: The Inside Story of the American Home.* Boston: Little, Brown, 1998.

Glass Window

Jütte, Daniel. *The Strait Gate: Thresholds and Power in Western History.* New Haven, CT: Yale University Press, 2015.

Melchoir-Bonnet, Sabine. *The Mirror: A History.* London: Routledge, 2002.

Parissien, Steven. *Interiors: The Home Since 1700.* London: Laurence King Publishing, 2008.

Sarti, Raffaella. *Europe at Home: Family and Material Culture, 1500–1800.* New Haven, CT: Yale University Press, 2004.

Thornton, Peter. *Authentic Decor: The Domestic Interior, 1620–1920.* London: Weldenfeld and Nicolson, 1984.

Tutton, Michael, Elizabeth Hirst, Hentie Louw, and Jill Pearce. *Windows: History, Repair and Conservation.* Hoboken, NJ: Taylor and Francis, 2015.

Globe

Goodman, Dena, and Kathryn Norberg. *Furnishing the Eighteenth Century: What Furniture Can Tell Us about the European and American Past.* New York: Routledge, 2011.

Jaffee, David. *A New Nation of Goods: The Material Culture of Early America.* Philadelphia, PA: University of Pennsylvania Press, 2012.

McMichael, Nancy, and David Emerick. *Snowdomes.* New York: Abbeville Press, 1990.

Pitchler, Britta. "Into the Wintry World of the Snow Globe: A Museum in Vienna Reveals the History of a Beloved Souvenir." *Los Angeles Times*, December 19, 2010.

Sumira, Sylvia. *The Art and History of the Globe.* London: The British Library, 2014.

Sumira, Sylvia. *Globes: 400 Years of Exploration, Navigation, and Power.* Chicago: The University of Chicago Press, 2014.

Ice Bucket

Dunne, Patrick. *The Epicurean Collector: Exploring the World of Culinary Antiques.* Boston: Little, Brown, 2002.

Glanville, Philippa, and Hilary Young. *Elegant Eating: Four Hundred Years of Dining in Style.* London: V & A Publications, 2002.

Paston-Williams, Sara. *The Art of Dining: A History of Cooking & Eating.* London: National Trust Limited, 1993.

von Drachenfels, Suzanne. *The Art of the Table: A Complete Guide to Table Setting, Table Manners, and Tableware.* New York: Simon & Schuster, 2008.

Incense

Aftel, Mandy. *Fragrant: The Secret Life of a Scent.* New York: Riverhead Books, 2014.

Classen, Constance, David Howes, and Anthony Synnott. *Aroma: The Cultural History of Smell.* New York: Routledge, 1994.

Le Guerer, Annick. *Scent: The Mysterious and Essential Powers of Smell.* New York: Kodansha America Inc., 1992.

Schiff, Stacy. *Cleopatra.* New York: Little, Brown and Co., 2010.

Jewelry Box

Currie, Elizabeth. *Inside the Renaissance House.* London: V & A Publications, 2006.

Linley, David. *Extraordinary Furniture.* London: Mitchell Beazley, 1996.

Jib Door

Boyer, Marie-France, and François Halard. *The Private Realm of Marie Antoinette.* London: Thames & Hudson, 2008.

Donato, Giuseppe, and Monique Seefried. *The Fragrant Past: Perfumes of Cleopatra and Julius Caesar.* Atlanta, GA: Emory University Museum of Art and Archaeology, 1989.

Hicks, Ashley. *David Hicks: A Life of Design.* New York: Rizzoli, 2009.

Hicks, David, with Nicholas Jenkins. *Living with Design.* New York: William Morrow and Company, 1979.

Lock and Key

Buehr, Walter. *The Story of Locks.* New York: Scribner, 1953.

Delalex, Hélène. *A Day with Marie Antoinette.* New York: Rizzoli, 2015.

Ekirch, A. Roger. *At Day's Close: Night in Times Past.* New York: Norton, 2006.

Jütte, Daniel. *The Strait Gate: Thresholds and Power in Western History.* New Haven, CT: Yale University Press, 2015.

Monk, Eric. *Keys: Their History and Collection.* Princes Risborough, UK: Shire, 2009.

Louis XVI Chair

Condon, Dianne Russell. *Jackie's Treasures: The Fabled Objects from the Auction of the Century.* New York: Clarkson Potter, 1996.

Delalex, Hélène. *A Day with Marie Antoinette.* New York: Rizzoli, 2015.

Farr, James. *The Work of France: Labor and Culture in Early Modern Times, 1350–1800.* Lanham, MD: Rowman & Littlefield, 2008.

Mattress

Beldegreen, Alecia. *The Bed.* New York: Stewart, Tabori & Chang, 1995.

Carlano, Anne, and Bobbie Sumberg. *Sleeping Around: The Bed from Antiquity to Now.* Seattle, WA: University of Washington Press, 2006.

Harris, Eileen. *Going to Bed.* London: V&A Museum, 1981.

Mirror

DeJean, Joan. *Essence of Style: How the French Invented High Fashion.* New York: Free Press, 2014.

Johnson, Steven. *How We Got to Now: Six Innovations That Made the Modern World*. London: Penguin, 2016.

Melchoir-Bonnet, Sabine. *The Mirror: A History*. London: Routledge, 2002.

Pendergrast, Mark. *Mirror Mirror: A History of the Human Love Affair with Reflections*. New York: Basic Books, 2004.

Phipps, Paula. *Mirrors: Reflections of Style*. New York: W.W. Norton, 2012.

Woods, May, and Arete Swartz Warren. *Glass Houses: A History of Greenhouses, Orangeries and Conservatories*. London: Aurum Press Ltd., 1988.

Monogram

Brumback, Cynthia. *The Art of the Monogram*. Orlando, FL: Story Farm, 2013.

Snodgrass, Mary Ellen. *World Clothing and Fashion: An Encyclopedia of History, Culture and Social Influence*. New York: Routledge, 2015.

Swan, Suzanne. *DK Eyewitness Travel Guide: Turkey*. New York: DK, 2016.

Whitman, Kimberly. *Monograms for the Home*. Layton, UT: Gibbs Smith, 2015.

Napkin

Fletcher, Nichola. *Charlemagne's Tablecloth: A Piquant History of Feasting*. New York: St. Martin's Press, 2014.

McIver, Katherine A. *Cooking and Eating in Renaissance Italy: From Kitchen to Table*. London: Rowman & Littlefield, 2015.

Strong, Roy. *Feast: A History of Grand Eating*. London: Jonathan Cape, 2002.

Parquet Floor

Fawcett, Jane, ed. *Historic Floors: Their History and Conservation*. Oxford, UK: Butterworth-Heinemann, 2001.

Miller, Judith. *Style Sourcebook*. London: Mitchell Beazley, 2003.

Piano

Ajmar-Wollheim, Marta, and Flora Dennis. *At Home in Renaissance Italy*. London: V & A Publications, 2006.

Closson, Ernest. *History of the Piano*. New York: St. Martin's Press, 1944.

Flanders, Judith. *Inside the Victorian Home: A Portrait of a Domestic Life in Victorian England*. New York: W.W. Norton, 2003.

Grover, David S. *The Piano: Its Story from Zither to Grand*. New York: Charles Scribner's Sons, 1978.

Hoover, Cynthia Adams, Patrick Rucker, and Edwin M. Good. *Piano 300: Celebrating Three Centuries of People and Pianos*. Washington, DC: National Museum of American History, 2001.

van Barthold, Kenneth, and David Buckton. *Story of the Piano*. London: British Broadcasting Corporation, 1975.

Picnic Basket

Fletcher, Nichola. *Charlemagne's Tablecloth: A Piquant History of Feasting*. New York: St. Martin's Press, 2014.

Latham, Jean. *The Pleasures of Your Company: A History of Manners and Meals*. London: Adam & Charles Black, 1972.

Levy, Walter. *The Picnic: A History*. Lanham, MD: AltaMira Press, 2014.

Snodgrass, Mary Ellen. *Encyclopedia of Kitchen History*. New York: Fitzroy Dearborn, 2004.

Pillow

Carlano, Anne, and Bobbie Sumberg. *Sleeping Around: The Bed from Antiquity to Now*. Seattle, WA: University of Washington Press, 2006.

Eden, Mary, and Richard Carrington. *The Philosophy of the Bed*. London: Hutchinson, 1961.

Morse, Edward S. *Japanese Homes and Their Surroundings*. London: Kegan Paul Ltd., 2005.

Wright, Malcolm. "Ceramic Pillows." *Studio Potter* 11, no. 1 (December 1982): 80–81.

Plate

Heugel, Inès. *Laying the Elegant Table: China, Faience, Porcelain, Majolica, Glassware, Flatware, Tureens, Platters, Trays, Centerpieces, Tea Sets*. New York: Rizzoli, 2006.

Riegler, Shax. *Dish: 813 Colorful, Wonderful Dinner Plates*. New York: Artisan, 2011.

Playing Cards

Beal, George. *Playing Cards and Their Story*. New York: Arco, 1975.

Epstein, Richard A. *The Theory of Gambling and Statistical Logic*. Burlington, MA: Academic Press, 2009.

Koda, Harold. *Dangerous Liaisons: Fashion and Furniture in the Eighteenth Century*. New York: Metropolitan Museum of Art, 2007.

Tilly, Roger. *Playing Cards: Pleasures and Treasures*. New York: G.P. Putman's Sons, 1967.

Wilkinson, W. H. "Chinese Origin of Playing Cards." *American Anthropologist* 8 (January 1895): 61–78.

Potpourri

Dugan, Holly. *The Ephemeral History of Perfume: Scent and Sense in Early Modern England*. Baltimore, MD: Johns Hopkins University Press, 2011.

Dullea, Georgia. "What's That Smell? Probably, It's Potpourri." *New York Times*, February 15, 1990.

Genders, Roy. *Perfume through the Ages*. New York: Putnam, 1972.

Punch Bowl

Barr, Andrew. *Drink: A Social History of America*. New York: Carroll & Graf, 2003.

Oliver, Charles, Paul Fishman, and Fiorella Busoni. *Dinner at Buckingham Palace: Based on the Diaries of Charles Oliver*. London: Metro, 2007.

Wondrich, David. *Imbibe*. New York: Penguin Publishing Group, 2015.

Wondrich, David. *Punch: The Delights (and Dangers) of the Flowing Bowl*. New York: Penguin Books, 2010.

Rocking Chair

Abbott, James A., and Elaine M. Rice. *Designing Camelot: The Kennedy White House Restoration*. New York: Van Nostrand Reinhold, 1998.

Rybczynski, Witold. *Now I Sit Me Down: From Klismos to Plastic Chair: A Natural History*. New York: Farrar, Straus and Giroux, 2016.

Steinbaum, Bernice. *The Rocker: An American Design Tradition*. New York: Rizzoli, 1992.

Rose

Aftel, Mandy. *Essence and Alchemy: A Book of Perfume*. New York: North Point Press, 2001.

Fletcher, Nichola. *Charlemagne's Tablecloth: A Piquant History of Feasting*. New York: St. Martin's Press, 2014.

Genders, Roy. *Perfume Through the Ages*. New York: Putnam, 1972.

Paterson, Allen. *The History of the Fragrant Rose*. London: Little Books, 2007.

Shower

Ashenburg, Katherine. *The Dirt on Clean: An Unsanitized History*. New York: Farrar, Straus and Giroux, 2014.

Picard, Liza. *Victorian London: The Tale of a City 1840–1870*. New York: St. Martin's Press, 2014.

Sparke, Penny. *Elsie de Wolfe: The Birth of Modern Interior Decoration*. New York: Acanthus Press, 2005.

Williamson, Jefferson. *The American Hotel: An Anecdotal History*. New York: Alfred A. Knopf, 1930.

Visser, Margaret. *The Way We Are: The Astonishing Anthropology of Everyday Life*. New York: Kodansha International, 1997.

Sofa

DeJean, Joan. *The Age of Comfort: When Paris Discovered Casual and the Modern Home Began*. New York: Bloomsbury Press, 2013.

Spoon

Bushman, Richard. *The Refinement of America: Persons, Houses, Cities*. New York: Alfred A. Knopf, 1992.

Heugel, Inès. *Laying the Elegant Table: China, Faience, Porcelain, Majolica, Glassware, Flatware, Tureens, Platters, Trays, Centerpieces, Tea Sets*. New York: Rizzoli, 2006.

Kean, Sam. *The Disappearing Spoon: And Other True Tales of Madness, Love, and the History of the World from the Periodic Table of the Elements*. London: Black Swan, 2011.

Morgan, Joan, and Elisabeth Dowle. *The Book of Pears: The Definitive History and Guide to Over 500 Varieties*. London: Ebury Press, 2015.

Snodgrass, Mary Ellen. *Encyclopedia of Kitchen History*. New York: Fitzroy Dearborn, 2004.

Visser, Margaret, and Bee Wilson. *The Rituals of Dinner: The Origins, Evolution, Eccentricities, and Meaning of Table Manners*. London: Penguin, 1991.

von Drachenfels, Suzanne. *The Art of the Table: A Complete Guide to Table Setting, Table Manners, and Tableware*. New York: Simon & Schuster, 2008.

Wilson, Bee, and Annabel Lee. *Consider the Fork: A History of How We Cook and Eat*. New York: Basic Books, 2013.

Tablecloth

Brandreth, Gyles Daubeney. *Book of Pears*. London: Pelham Books, 1979.

Fletcher, Nichola. *Charlemagne's Tablecloth: A Piquant History of Feasting*. New York: St. Martin's Press, 2014.

Hollingsworth, Mary. *The Cardinal's Hat: Money, Ambition and Housekeeping in a Renaissance Court*. London: Profile Books, 2004.

Tassel

Baird, Rosemary. *Mistress of the House: Great Ladies and Grand Houses, 1670–1830*. London: Weidenfeld & Nicolson, 2003.

Letheren, Emma. *An Investigation into Passementerie: A Focused Study of the Tassel to Establish a Rigorous Compilation of Definitions and Classifications, Leading to a Personal Creative Exploration.* Dissertation, University of Wolverhampton, 2003.

Levron, Jacques. *Daily Life in Versailles in the Seventeenth and Eighteenth Centuries.* New York: The Macmillan Company, 1968.

Miller, Judith. *Style Sourcebook.* London: Mitchell Beazley, 2003.

Welch, Nancy. *Tassels: The Fanciful Embellishment.* Asheville, NC: Lark Books, 1992.

Teapot

Flanders, Judith. *Inside the Victorian Home: A Portrait of Domestic Life in Victorian England.* New York: W.W. Norton, 2006.

Heugel, Inès. *Laying the Elegant Table: China, Faience, Porcelain, Majolica, Glassware, Flatware, Tureens, Platters, Trays, Centerpieces, Tea Sets.* New York: Rizzoli, 2006.

Lethbridge, Lucy. *Servants: A Downstairs View of Twentieth-Century Britain.* London: Bloomsbury Publishing, 2013.

Sweet, Fay. *Alessi: Art and Pottery.* London: Thames and Hudson, 1998.

von Drachenfels, Suzanne. *The Art of the Table: A Complete Guide to Table Setting, Table Manners, and Tableware.* New York: Simon & Schuster, 2008.

Tented Room

Chevallier, Bernard. *Empire Splendor: French Taste in the Age of Napoleon.* New York: Vendome Press, 2008.

DeLorme, Eleanor P. *Josephine and the Arts of the Empire.* Los Angeles, CA: J. Paul Getty Museum, 2005.

Tile

Faas, Patrick. *Around the Roman Table: Food and Feasting in Ancient Rome.* Chicago: University of Chicago Press, 2005.

Herbert, Tony, and Kathryn Huggins. *The Decorative Tile in Architecture and Interiors.* London: Phaidon Press, 1995.

Lang, Gordon. *1000 Tiles: Ten Centuries of Decorative Ceramics.* San Francisco, CA: Chronicle Books, 2004.

van Lemmen, Hans. *Tiles in Architecture.* London: Laurence King Publishing, 1993.

Tolix Marais A Chair

Durieux, Brigitte, Laziz Hamani, and Elodie Palasse-Leroux. *Industrial Chic: 50 Icons of Furniture and Lighting Design.* New York: Abrams, 2012.

Durieux, Brigitte. *Tolix.* Paris: Martinière, 2008.

Topiary

James, Peter, and Nick Thorpe. *Ancient Inventions.* New York: Ballantine Books, 1995.

Lablaude, Pierre-André. *The Gardens of Versailles.* Paris: Editions Scala, 2005.

Moss, Charlotte. "The Eloquence of Silence." *New York Times*, January 12, 2014.

Trestle Table

Snodgrass, Mary Ellen. *Encyclopedia of Kitchen History.* New York: Fitzroy Dearborn, 2004.

Turkish and Persian Rugs

Ajmar-Wollheim, Marta, and Flora Dennis. *At Home in Renaissance Italy*. London: V & A Publications, 2006.

Brantôm, Pierre de Bourdeille. *Lives of Fair and Gallant Ladies*. London: The Alexandrian Society, 1922.

Goldstone, Nancy Bazelon. *The Rival Queens: Catherine de' Medici, Her Daughter Marguerite de Valois, and the Betrayal That Ignited a Kingdom*. London: Weidenfeld & Nicholson, 2016.

James, Peter, and Nick Thorpe. *Ancient Inventions*. New York: Ballantine Books, 1995.

Milanesi, Enza. *The Carpet: An Illustrated Guide to the Rugs and Kilims of the World*. London: I. B. Tauris & Co. Ltd., 1999.

Prioleau, Betsy. *Seductress: Women Who Ravished the World and Their Lost Art of Love*. New York: Viking, 2003.

Thorndike, Joseph Jacobs. *The Magnificent Builders and Their Dream Houses*. New York: American Heritage Publishing Co., 1978.

Vase

Berrall, Julia S. *A History of Flower Arrangement*. London: Saint Austin Press, 1997.

Blacker, Mary Rose. *Flora Domestica: A History of British Flower Arranging, 1500–1930*. New York: Harry N. Abrams, 2000.

Gere, Charlotte, and Marina Vaizey. *Great Women Collectors*. London: P. Wilson, 1999.

Wallpaper

Brunet, Genevieve. *The Wallpaper Book*. London: Thames & Hudson, 2012.

de Dampierre, Florence, Tim Street-Porter, and Pieter Estersohn. *Walls: Mural, Wood Panel, Stencil, Wallpaper*. New York: Rizzoli, 2011.

Hoskins, Lesley, ed. *The Papered Wall: The History, Patterns and Techniques of Wallpaper*. London: Thames & Hudson, 2005.

Thibaut-Pomerantz, Carolle. *Wallpaper: A History of Styles and Trends*. Paris: Flammarion, 2009.

Windsor Chair

de Dampierre, Florence. *Chairs: A History*. New York: Harry N. Abrams, 2006.

Evans, Nancy Goyne. *Windsor-Chair Making in America: From Craft Shop to Consumer*. Hanover, NH: University Press of New England, 2006.

Harding-Hill, Michael. *Windsor Chairs: An Illustrated Celebration*. Woodbridge: Antique Collectors' Club, 2003.

Wineglass

Ashton, Kevin. *How to Fly a Horse: The Secret History of Creation, Invention and Discovery*. London: Windmill Books, 2016.

Brears, Peter. *Cooking and Dining in Medieval England*. Blackawton, UK: Prospect Books, 2012.

Brown, Patricia Fortini. *Private Lives in Renaissance Venice: Art, Architecture, and the Family*. New Haven, CT: Yale University Press, 2004.

Bull, Donald, and Joseph C. Paradi. *Wine Antiques & Collectibles*. Atglen, PA: Schiffer Publishing Ltd., 2013.

Hollingsworth, Mary. *The Cardinal's Hat: Money, Ambition and House-keeping in a Renaissance Court*. London: Profile Books, 2004.

Zerwick, Chloe. *A Short History of Glass*. New York: Corning Museum of Glass, 1980.

Wreath and Garland

Classen, Constance, David Howes, and Anthony Synnott. *Aroma: The Cultural History of Smell*. New York: Routledge, 1994.

Lynn, David Brandon. *Daughters and Parents: Past, Present, and Future*. Monterey, CA: Brooks/Cole Publishing Co., 1979.

Smith, Georgiana Reynolds. *Table Decoration: Yesterday, Today & Tomorrow*. Japan: Charles E. Tuttle Co. Inc., 1968.